Cancer Fight

MY WIFE'S FAITHFUL, FEARLESS BATTLE AGAINST BREAST CANCER

D1603099

Michael Coccari

MICHAEL COCCARI

Copyright © 2020 by Michael Coccari

Paperback: 978-1-953731-97-5
eBook: 978-1-953731-96-8
Library of Congress Control Number: 2020934770

All rights reserved. No part of this publication may be reproduced, distributed, or transmitted in any form or by any electronic or mechanical means, without the prior written permission of the publisher, except in the case of brief quotations embodied in critical reviews and certain other noncommercial uses permitted by copyright law.

This is a work of nonfiction.

Ordering Information:

BookTrail Agency
8838 Sleepy Hollow Rd.
Kansas City, MO 64114

Printed in the United States of America

Table of Contents

To Darlene Rae Coccari—my eternal wife, life partner, and fearless cancer warrior:

for teaching me
to see,
to feel,
to know,
to care,
to love,
to live,
to appreciate,
to fight,
to withstand,
to endure,
to overcome,
to accept.

Acknowledgements

M y list of people and organizations to thank will inevitably be flawed by omissions. That said, here it goes.

For providing Darlene with excellent medical care and treatment, I want to thank the oncologists as well as the Infusion Center nurses and staff of the CBCC (Comprehensive Blood and Cancer Center) in Bakersfield, California. I also want to thank the doctors, nurses, and staff of Memorial Hospital in Bakersfield.

For providing Darlene with love and support, I want to thank the staff and students of the Mojave Unified School District in Mojave, California. I especially want to acknowledge Darlene's teaching colleagues and spiritual sisters Kris Zonn, Mary DeBoard, Stephanie Peet, Debbie Root, Ruth Boetel, Karen Day, and Marilyn Berg.

Darlene would want me to emphasize how grateful she always was for her lifelong friends Elizabeth Mardis, Rose Zerda, Tracy Keller, Ty Zeretzke, and Chloe Bussiere.

For providing me with empathy and understanding, I would like to thank the staff and students of Arvin High School in Arvin, California. I especially want to acknowledge my teaching colleagues Cynthia Brakeman, Kimberly Lee, Jay Campbell, Kacie Ponce, Krystal Laster, Amanda Smith, John Rose, Diane Trihey, Carol Lee, Robert Ruckman, and Tonya Davis. I also want to thank my administrators for their support. These include principal Ed Watts, retired principal Carlos Sardo, assistant principals Robert Moore and Brandi Ball, former discipline dean Stephen Granucci, instructional dean Rocío Cantú, athletic director Ralph Gonzales, activities director Jessica Sinden, and counselor Cynthia Zamora.

I am eternally appreciative of my sister Judy and her husband Roger Hough for their compassion.

For starting a Tehachapi Relay-for-Life team in honor of Darlene, I want to express my deep thanks to Debbie and Larry Root.

I will be forever grateful to Jackie Wood of Jackie Wood Photography in Tehachapi, California for the beautiful photos she produced of Darlene.

I would also like to acknowledge the care and support of OneLegacy's donor family aftercare department and Science Care, a medical research organization in Phoenix, Arizona.

INTRODUCTION

A Prayer

I offer these words as a prayer that I will have the strength to know you as you deserve to be known. I offer these words as a testament to the honor and grace with which you have led your life, especially during the years that you have been so directly threatened by the merciless enemy called cancer. I offer these words as a reflection of my desire to care for you in the manner you have a right to be cared for. Knowing that these words will helplessly expose the vast gap between the care you deserve and the care I have been able to provide, I offer them as an apology for what my heart could only imagine but not fully express.

You are the toughest and bravest person I have ever known, and I can do nothing more important with my life than try to document why this is so. Your toughness and bravery are all the more noteworthy for being contextualized in a personality that is wholly without ego, arrogance, or presumption. You are minus any instinct to self-aggrandize or call any attention whatsoever to your attitudes and actions. I marvel with ever-increasing astonishment at your decency, humility, optimism, and faith in a just and merciful God, in spite of the toll breast cancer has exacted over the last six years.

Some of what follows was written during the dark hours when we both should have been sleeping. Instead, you fight tirelessly and undauntedly against the cancer that nightly invades your bed, your consciousness, and your dreams with the same ferociousness that it has invaded your body's cells. Instead, I lie near you on the floor or sit in a wretched heap, praying, longing for relief to come to you, hugging you with my arms, mind, and soul, and sometimes writing to honor you, to more fully express my love for you, and to make sense of it all.

CHAPTER ONE

Cancer Chooses You with Random Precision

Married female, with no history of cancer in her family.
Cancer doesn't care.

Age forty-four, mentally and physically healthy and vibrant, emotionally and physically loving and positive, graceful and humble, possessing an infallibly affirming attitude, in love with life.
Cancer doesn't care.

Loving mother to two beautiful sons, ages nineteen and ten.
Cancer doesn't care.

Loving daughter to salt-of-the-earth Indiana parents.
Cancer doesn't care.

Loving sister to three loving, rugged brothers.
Cancer doesn't care.

Loyal friend, treating all people as sisters and brothers in the true spirit of Jesus.
Cancer doesn't care.

Collegiate tennis scholarship recipient, with a killer, whipping backhand.
Cancer doesn't care.

Beloved elementary school teacher, exhibiting special dedication to those lost and damaged souls who desperately need love and guidance.
Cancer doesn't care.

Former government employee, with security clearance for classified operations.
Cancer doesn't care.

My loving wife.
Cancer doesn't care.

We leave the oncologist's office with a referral to the surgeon who would cut away your breasts. You had already said goodbye to them before we reached the car. Breasts are only breasts. Life is not only life. It is the lives of your sons too, and your thoughts are focused squarely on them. How will we tell them? What details will we leave out to minimize the shock and give them time to process the frightening information?

Cancer is not possessed by a conscience. Cancer is not possessed by faith in God. Maybe we have an edge.

The Buddhist teaching about how to respond to a poisonous arrow in one's body helped us understand how to move forward. Why a poison-tipped arrow found you mattered not at all. Removing the arrow and all its poison was the only subject worthy of our attention. Endless questioning of fate and chance was pointless. Scholarly, metaphysical discussions, enticing and intriguing in the abstract, were foolhardy in reality. Why cancer chose you was irrelevant. Allowing us to become mired in the harsh details of the disease would lead only to depression and inaction. The arrow needed to be removed. In our own minds and with our sons foremost in our thoughts, we needed to emphasize the plan to deal with the poisoned arrow. The oncologist would treat, diminish, and halt the spreading poison. The surgeon would remove the arrow. We needed to make sure that we all stayed focused on the plan rather than the cause.

The arrow is just an arrow. We would think of it and treat it aggressively as such.

CHAPTER TWO

A False Sense of Security

Your first and controlling instinct, upon detecting a lump in your left breast while showering, was to dismiss it and resume normal life. You had me feel the lump immediately; you were curious but unconcerned. As I felt the small mass, about the size of a golf ball and located centrally on the side of your breast, I began to panic. You saw the worry in my face and quickly instructed me to relax. The mass felt too hard to me for me to ignore it as easily as you intended to.

For as long as I have known you, you have consistently displayed an enviable and exemplary ability to compartmentalize events and conditions in your life and to maintain proportionality of emotion in a way that I have never been able to emulate. This ability has allowed you to function normally under circumstances that typically bring my life to a standstill and consume me to the point of dysfunction.

Prior to discovering the foreign mass, we were headed to a professional baseball game for a weekend getaway. After detecting the mass, you argued that there was no reason to alter our plans. You were calmly insistent. In contrast, I was upset, beside myself, at a loss for how to proceed with normalcy of attitude and action. You matter-of-factly assured me that the lump would turn out to be a cyst, no doubt about it; you had had them before. In your mind, the lump was no big deal, nothing to be concerned about, no reason to let the discovery occupy inordinate attention or distract us from our plans. You would schedule a mammogram as soon as we were back from our outing.

Attending the game, we were like any other fan—sitting and cheering the Los Angeles Angels, absorbing and getting lost in the green, pastoral island of escape amid Orange County's suburban, conflagrated morass of bodies, buildings, signage, and freeways; ignoring life's press of duties, deadlines, and deals. You showed with utter confidence no worry about the mass of interloping tissue that had formed in your left breast. You had convincingly relegated it to the pedestrian status of cyst, and I weakly went along with your judgment, in mental anguish, emotional discomfort, and general hesitation, all of which I struggled to conceal from you.

During the game, you retreated from an unmerciful sun to shaded seats, happy to sacrifice your proximity to the field for coolness. I held out for a few innings, unwilling to yield my chance at a foul ball along the left field foul line, only two rows from grass. The blazing sun was a secondary concern. The foreign tissue in your breast controlled my thoughts. I was happy to have you behind me, unable to see my concern, afraid that it would hinder your calmness.

Of course I had no clue what was really going on in your mind. I only had the external evidence, which I acknowledge often misleads. When I finally rejoined you, unwilling to spend the entire game apart, you were engaged in smooth conversation with your seatmates— an elderly couple who were faithful and extremely knowledgeable Angel fans. They were, in your mind, such an adorable couple; they appeared to be in their late seventies, but their minds were alighted with bubbling energy and obvious love for each other. The couple alternated sentences as they informed us that they lived minutes from the ballpark and took in about fifty games each year. You looked at me, and I knew instantly what you were thinking: could we one day be so lucky as to retire somewhere in Anaheim and be able to root for the Angels as often as our newfound friends? Living in Tehachapi, we felt fortunate to be able to see one or two games during an average summer.

Understanding nods, quiet smiles, and a sense that life couldn't be better at that moment ruled the collective mood of our contented foursome. If you were preoccupied with what could be reigning in your left breast, you kept it hidden.

Our ride home was nothing more than a satisfied ending to a perfect weekend escape. Your outward demeanor indicated that we were not riding toward an MRI or CAT scan. We were simply going home, grateful for a perfect weekend, mentally lingering in our pleasurable respite as lucky baseball fans. The Angels had won. Once home, you would schedule a mammogram; the doctor would confirm the lump as a cyst, and it would be dissolved with medication, as had occurred in the past.

Driving the roughly three hours from Anaheim to Tehachapi, I used an inordinate amount of strength to conceal my restlessness in the car seat. I kept telling myself over and over to trust in your certainty that the only thing waiting for us at home was a report of a cyst in your left breast, which would be treated either with medication to dissolve it or, at worst, with outpatient surgery to remove it. I wanted with all my might to refrain from sending any negative energy or doubt your way. Those three hours seemed like three days to me.

CHAPTER THREE

Reality Intervenes

The oncologist's words pop like firecrackers: Breast cancer, stage 4, incalculably aggressive. Hormonal cause. Estrogen has apparently betrayed you. Yours is an invasive cancer, meaning that it has spread beyond your breast into surrounding tissue, lymph nodes, and possibly organs. Must start chemotherapy immediately. Yesterday would have been better. Tomorrow is almost too late.

The oncologist's eyes are impossibly wide and unblinking, as are yours, as are mine.

Meaning descends: sinister intent, lethal effect. The cliché "Life changes in an instant" demands payment in full.

The firecrackers continue popping: Of course, a mastectomy will be scheduled. One breast for sure; bilateral might be the smarter, precautionary decision, if you agree to that. Lymph nodes will also need to be removed, along with a certain amount of tissue and muscle as well. Won't know how many nodes and how much tissue and muscle until the surgeon gets inside to see with his eyes and feel with his fingers. Scans only reveal so much.

Shouldn't we drop the guillotine first? Get rid of the disease with a dramatic strike? Why are we scheduling chemotherapy prior to surgery? You understandably want the cancer removed, not treated. Get the poison out of your body immediately.

More firecrackers: The cancer is too entrenched and moving much too fast to perform surgery before beginning chemotherapy.

Get at least one treatment in. Then surgery. Scheduling surgery before chemo would allow the cancer to continue spreading undeterred while you take time that your body does not have to recover from the surgery.

The words *stage 4* ricochet violently and endlessly within the claustrophobic exam room.

No time for you to apprehend the meaning, which might have been a good thing. Concentrate on the treatment instead of on the problem. Focus on the arrow. That's what I thought. I will never know what actually went through your mind at the time.

I know the news hit me with the force of a lightning strike to my solar plexus. I don't know how to describe how the news hit you. I know what I saw in your eyes. You were shaken to the core of your core. You were in a state of disbelief. Yet, yet, you were making sure you saw your faith in another world imprinted on everything in this world. You were deciding exactly where your foot would come down off the exam table to maintain your balance and set a tone for all succeeding steps. You were already saying goodbye to breasts and nipples and whatever lymph nodes, tissues, and muscles the cancer had ruined beyond recovery. You were looking at me and tacitly asking if I would be strong enough and faithful enough to meet the challenges ahead.

CHAPTER FOUR

No Cartoon

Even as a child, I never spent much time watching cartoons. But in the immediate aftermath of receiving the oncologist's diagnosis of your stage 4 invasive breast cancer, I inexplicably have cartoon images in my subconscious mind.

What comes into view is a cartoonish wobbling of a manhole cover, comically cascading into place. Sound echoes in unison with the viewer's laughter, flattening and burying some hopeless figure, a *Mr. Magoo* type, consisting of and consumed by desperate yet hilarious notions and actions. In my mind's eye, the cartoon victim has found himself beneath a falling manhole cover and is about to be pancaked beyond recognition. The scene finalizes a much anticipated and enjoyed escapade of humor and absurdity, with the built-in solace of knowing it will be repeated again, right after the commercial, and no one will have experienced a moment's worth of pain, much less injury or death. The violence explodes as all wildly erratic movement and innocent innuendo, lacking lethality. No one is really hurt or even bruised much. All will rise again—body, mind, and soul intact, ever fearless and hopeful, ready for the next thrilling adventure.

But the scene engulfing us as an immense, fearful, frightening wave is regrettably no cartoon. Comedy and entertainment have become foreign and useless. Sound, especially laughter, has been muted. Desperation remains, but it lacks the subtlest hint of charm, humor, or innocence; instead, it drills, burns, and obliterates all sense of safety and escape.

The scene played out in the oncologist's office was as far from a cartoon as imaginable. We never anticipated it, and any possibility of enjoyment has been forever factored out. Absurdity reigns, but it indiscriminately drips acid. The violence seems conscious, intentional, and infinite in its capacity to seek and destroy. Fear rages and hope appears now on an endangered emotions list.

Welcome to your life.

The wobbling, echoing manhole cover turns out to be a metaphor for the endless hours and days that we wait for the phone to ring, or more hopefully, for the phone not to ring. Upon our return from our baseball trip, you had a mammogram and an MRI. After these tests, we were told to wait for the results. If we never received a phone call, that meant everything was fine. If we received a call, that meant trouble. The manhole cover wobbled in my mind for seven days. The phone didn't ring. We thought you were free and clear of trouble. On the seventh day, we came home to find a message from your doctor's nurse on our answering machine. You had an appointment scheduled for the very next day, at 8:00 a.m. The continuously revolving, wobbling, echoing manhole cover finally descended with destructive purpose. You are directly beneath its ugly force; I, only indirectly, but even that is too much. Whatever cartoon qualities I have imagined linger only to annoy, ridicule, mock. This scene is all too dramatic, with tragedy I no longer have to imagine lurking ruinously.

The waiting for you lasted for an interminable, tortuous time. You alternated between thoughts of having dodged a bullet and thoughts of utter doom. You felt your life changing even as you tried to convince yourself that nothing had changed. You played the message over and over again, trying to discern urgency or nonchalance in the nurse's tone of voice. You implored me to listen to the message with you and analyze what I heard. My efforts to ease your fears failed and eventually irritated you. The message was, after all, for you, not me.

Your life, and mine to a far lesser extent, has suddenly become something infected with sinister and seething toxicity; we are wholly without the need for vicarious threat and thrill. An enemy named breast cancer has found you out, and it has arrived in a most unfriendly and pernicious mood.

CHAPTER FIVE

Abstractions No More

Strange things happen when a doctor introduces the words *breast cancer* to a conversation. His eyes enlarge. His blinking stops or delays unnaturally. A moment of full ocular contact ensues, his eyes registering shock and concern. Sympathy? Pity? Then his eyes seek refuge in inanimate objects or empty space, anywhere away from the patient. Perhaps he is most acutely aware of his Hippocratic oath at such a moment. Perhaps he is reevaluating his decision to enter medical school and wondering if he is equal to the task at hand: delivering the news that no one is ever ready to hear.

Your test results confirm that the mass in your breast is cancerous. While delivering that news, his voice becomes almost inaudible, as if the words themselves are too awful to articulate fully. His eyes try not to reveal a future forever changed, but they fail. His life is forever altered for merely uttering the words. The patient's life . . . well . . . the patient's life has been redefined from the cellular level up through every whim, wish, wonder, wander. The invasion extends beyond the physical into the mental, emotional, spiritual, and sixth-sensical.

The strangeness within the now-strangling confines of the doctor's exam room (in the spirit of Richard III, "My kingdom for a window") extends to the doctor's breathing. He inhales perceptibly, dramatically, and oh so empathically. His exhale seems never to occur.

The physician seems to be aware that his every mannerism, gesture, facial expression, eye movement, and weight shift are being read, dissected, analyzed, interpreted. Perhaps the doctor needs nearly as much as you, the patient, an escape hatch. None abides.

My shock at hearing the medical verdict of breast cancer is more profound than any I have ever experienced. This shock will soon be surpassed. My English teacher persona, habitually thinking of analogies, kicks in as I try to comprehend the full meaning of what has just occurred. Your doctor has sent you into the Ardennes Forest in WWII. You are under siege, underdressed, underarmed, outnumbered, and exposed to perpetual winter. He has sent you into the tunnels of Vietnam in the 1960s, where air hides and the enemy resides. No mercy, no retreat, no reconsideration. He has sent you into the boxing ring to fight Muhammad Ali in his prime. Your opponent's glare decimates, his words demean, and his gloves destroy. He has sent you with General Custer in the 1870s, and Custer is commanding you deeper into the valley of the Little Bighorn River.

These abstractions are thin shadows of your new reality.

Despite all, I am not surprised that you have maintained your balance on the exam bench. You appear steadier and more resilient than I could ever hope to be. You are not wasting physical movement, and you are beginning to ask questions. I am shifting weight and crossing and uncrossing my legs pointlessly.

Emotionally saturated, the conversation has become transactional. You are being treated at the Comprehensive Blood and Cancer Center (CBCC) of Bakersfield, close to our home in Tehachapi, California. It is affiliated with UCLA, a state-of-the-art treatment center, obviating the need to travel out of the area for consultation and treatment. Your oncologist assures us that he and his own family would seek help at the CBCC.

The doctor exits the exam room to make arrangements for your first chemotherapy treatments. We sit in stunned silence, still absorbing, comprehending, and realizing the "cyst certainty" theory has been mercilessly crushed. The air continues to stifle. The exam room continues to constrict.

You make it clear that I cannot hug you right now. A hug will initiate a collapse of composure, resiliency, and confidence.

We tacitly agree to fight. As you are not a fan of Sylvester Stallone's film persona, the boxer Rocky Balboa, I dare not utter the pugilist's hesitant statement in the first film as he anticipates entering the ring against the mighty Apollo Creed: "I'll fight the fight." If cancer is Apollo Creed, and you, my beloved wife, are Rocky, we have a chance.

CHAPTER SIX

Infusion Center

We are going to a place called the Infusion Center as part of the Comprehensive Blood and Cancer Center in Bakersfield, California. There, you will receive your first chemotherapy treatment. Your oncologist informed us that your breast cancer was so hyperaggressive that one or two treatments needed to be done prior to your scheduled bilateral mastectomy surgery. Performing surgery first would necessitate a lengthy recovery period that you could not afford without chemo already in your system, counterattacking the cancer cells.

Psychologically, I don't know how one simultaneously prepares for the double onslaught of chemotherapy and surgery. Preparing for one would be enough of a burden. Both at once seems absurd. For you, the knowledge that something is now being done stands as a saving grace. You are no longer an unknowing, passive, defenseless victim. We have a plan that is about to begin. Your anxiousness to go on offense against cancer mitigates the intense psychological trauma of both chemo and surgery.

You are naturally focused on how the chemotherapy treatment will be conducted. You are concentrating on where to go and questioning in your mind the actual protocol. The name of the center is of no interest to you whatsoever. I, on the other hand, am intrigued by the name *Infusion Center*. The connotation suggests a spa-like experience. The true meaning of the center with such a delicate name softens into something wholesome, assuaging, nurturing, and restorative, such as a full-body massage or some exotic skin treatment involving mud and hot rocks.

What exactly will be infused into your bloodstream is so diabolically toxic that it would kill a buffalo or grizzly bear if administered in the wrong dosage. The name *Infusion Center*, I suppose, is intended to disguise or at least distract from that reality. I am thankful that none of my musings on the center's name register on your mental radar as we report for treatment. I resist the urge to share my thoughts with you. Instead, I try to be as tacitly supportive of your ordeal as possible, knowing that you need to concentrate, like an athlete, on the task at hand. Musings from spectators serve only as an unnecessary annoyance.

We are surprised at how many cancer patients are spread throughout several large rooms. The patients are situated in recliners that are much better than rigid seats but still imbue an institutional aura that I cannot overlook. Translucent bags hang from freestanding IV-drip poles that occupy the place where a reading lamp would be if we were at home instead of in a medical center. Nurse stations are centered in the rooms, and portable carts with trays and cabinets are in abundance. The nurses sit in front of computers when they are not attending to patients. They move around the rooms deftly, even as they communicate with one another about patients or casual topics. The nurses clearly run these rooms with great care, efficiency, and dexterity. Doctors are absent; physician's assistants sometimes filter through, usually holding paperwork, sometimes writing prescriptions as they chat with patients. But the nurses are in charge. When the machines beep and buzz, they respond and press the right buttons. They monitor the bags of chemo and antinausea medicine, insert the IVs in arms or port-a-caths, direct traffic in and out of the rooms, and print and supply medical reports when asked for by patients.

Most patients have a caregiver sitting with them on cushioned stackable seats or, occasionally, on round stools. A few patients are alone.

Some patients exhibit stoicism in their facial expressions and physical demeanor. These individuals talk in whispers or low tones with their loved ones who sit nearby. Some patients busy themselves with reading books or magazines; some knit or fill out note cards. Some simply sit quietly with eyes alert but usually avoiding eye contact with other patients. Some patients chat in an upbeat manner with nurses about children, the weather, and other casual topics.

Other patients display suffering in all its inglorious misery. These patients are dramatic in their facial expressions and physical demeanor. They tell heartbreaking stories in their tortured countenances. One look at them reveals the full force of cancer's attack. Their faces are twisted in pain and suffering. For some, just getting into the recliner proves agonizingly hard. They require assistance from loved ones and nurses. Once in the chair, they struggle to find a comfortable position. Often, they painfully reposition themselves without end. Some sigh and moan and cry out in pain. Some require oxygen; some need constant attention from a nurse. Loved ones present seem beside themselves to find a way to help.

We are struck by the patients' diversity of ages. Cancer does not discriminate based on age. We see elderly patients who need walkers or wheelchairs to move. Their arms are nearly as translucent as the chemo bags. We see a plethora of middle-aged patients. Most are dressed in the clothing of the chronically ill: T-shirts, sweats, shorts, and slippers. We see a rugged-looking middle-aged man wearing a UPS uniform.

In one corner, we notice what appears to be a junior high student being treated as his father sits by his side. The father looks sadder to me than his son. His son appears stoic, muscling up to the infusion of chemo. The father looks forlorn and devastated. Neither one of us can steal a second glance, fearing that we will lose our already tenuous composure.

We quickly learn the protocol. Before treatment, you have a blood draw to check your levels of white and red blood cells, platelets, as well as other components of your blood. If the data indicate that you are strong enough to endure the chemo treatment, the process begins. A nurse escorts us to an open recliner. Once seated, a nurse's assistant asks if you would like a warm blanket. As in the typical medical room or hospital, the temperature is on the chilly side, so a warm blanket is most welcome. We take off your shoes and elevate your legs. You are as comfortable as you can be under the circumstances. Your nurse begins to give you an antinausea infusion before the actual chemotherapy. Your nurse informs us that this medicine significantly reduces the incidences of vomiting or diarrhea.

Your nurse is informative, attentive, and caring. The antinausea medicine takes about thirty minutes. The drip seems surprisingly quick. Your infusion of chemo drugs takes much longer, the drip noticeably slower. I have given you magazines, water, and a candy bar. You are alert and chatting happily with your nurse and patients around you. I am grateful that the process is pain-free and efficient.

CHAPTER SEVEN

Warrior

You are a warrior. Warrior status is deserved first for your capacity to love life under cancer's unremitting attack. I cannot count or properly document how many friends and strangers have remarked to me about your positive outlook. They stand in wonder at the resiliency of your attitude, at the depth of your self-awareness, and at the strength of your self-composure. I usually say, when people's verbal and tacit expressions of disbelief and wonder turn in my direction, looking for an explanation, that your grace and fortitude form an indestructible monument that I feel privileged to witness and admire.

Before cancer, you loved life. You loved every second of life, even the trying ones. After cancer, you love life, more if that is possible, and every second is a trying one. Before cancer, you were eternally grateful to be alive. That is a cliché that I have rarely seen lived consistently in the flesh. After cancer, you are grateful to be alive, and the cliché has transformed into the most profound act of living I have ever observed firsthand.

You have stared *stage 4* in the eyes, unflinching, undaunted, undeterred, unwilling to back down, unwilling to succumb.

I don't know what has more crushing weight than a cancer diagnosis. Yet this heavy burden that you bear is mostly invisible. Somehow, you retain a lightness of spirit and an undiminished appreciation for life. You joke, you tease, you exaggerate, you exonerate, you laugh, you dance, you absorb all the goodness of each good moment, and you embody all the grace and ease of nature that would be more understandable in cancer's absence.

You are my present-day George Washington, given your own version of his formidable task to unite disparate troops, face overwhelming odds, and create an army of belief and courage from rags, farm rifles, and field horses.

In your version of Washington's challenge, with cancer the clear-eyed, determined enemy, you must unite the best qualities from your childhood in Indiana, your college and young adulthood in Texas, and your maturation in California, pulling together only the experiences that matter when existence has been redefined by evil threat and unrelenting attack. You never anticipated such an overwhelming task as facing cancer; never imagined that your resolve and coping mechanisms would be tested so relentlessly.

You are excavating latent strength buried in years of comfort and normalcy. You are embracing confrontation; you are developing a love of fighting. You are learning to live with unending threat; you are learning to fearlessly and hopefully turn every corner where death may be waiting.

The oncologist looks at you to deliver the news that your breast has been invaded, the nipple is surrounded, the tissue throughout the breast irreversibly compromised, the damage extending into the lymph nodes. Sacrifices will have to be made. Saving the soul will be at the expense of one breast, both if you want to be proactive, as well as muscles in your chest cavity and beneath your left arm.

Throughout my body, I can feel my blood panicking. I feel stabbing pains, imaginary swords slicing and piercing my flesh. I wonder when my body bypassed the innocent tingling of pins and needles.

You sit on the exam table, calm, focused, steady. You are without need to ponder or question. "When do we do this? How do we do this?" You are resolute—both breasts, no deliberation, no doubt. "Let's get on with it. Yesterday is not soon enough."

I don't think we ever uttered the words, but I know what we were both thinking, "At least we don't have to wait for the phone to ring anymore."

In the abstract, I have read many times of the need to control one's fear at the moment of threat in order to think clearly and act decisively. The abstract is so safe. My indulgence in reading literature and philosophy offers such a naive refuge from never actually taking a stand when the enemy comes knocking. Or for taking only hypothetical stands. You were not given such refuge, such hypothetical safe ground. An enemy with lethal intent is confronting you. An enemy has chosen you for a most unmerciful invasion. At your moment of attack, when refuge and hypotheticals ceased to exist, you held your ground, controlled your fear, thought clearly, and acted decisively.

A patriot to precious life.

Warrior.

CHAPTER EIGHT

Needles and Drips

W e are in the Infusion Center for your second chemotherapy treatment. Your first intravenous bag once again is an antinausea mixture that drips in an excruciatingly slow manner. I am counting to five before the next drip falls. The nurse, a different one from the first treatment, informs us that the medicine will reduce, though probably not eliminate, the degree of the side effects chemo usually causes. According to our nurse, twenty years ago, a patient undergoing chemo invariably had to endure extreme exhaustion, rampant diarrhea, vomiting, constipation, aborted appetite, loss of hair, and as Mark Twain would say, "general miserableness." Today, those side effects remain, albeit thankfully to a lesser degree due to the antinausea medicine. Chemo is still the main weapon in the cancer war, but its aim has improved, and its side effects have been controlled. The nurse warns us that we will have to see how you respond to the treatment; each person reacts differently.

The bag of chemo replaces the antinausea medicine some forty-five minutes later. Your legs and feet are comfortably elevated by the recliner's footrest. The nurse has brought you a warm blanket and a pillow, which ameliorates the institutional coldness. You have collapsible tray tables on either side of your chair. I am sitting restively in a hard- back chair next to you.

The chemo mixture flows much more swiftly. I can barely count to one before the next drip falls. After initially surveying the room and noting the other patients' ages, you have withdrawn into yourself. The blanket and pillow have made you feel comfortable enough to fall asleep.

After the initial needle draw of blood to check your vital stats and then the insertion of the IV in your arm, which becomes the onramp into your veins for the drugs, you have been without physical pain. You have mercifully never had a fear of needles. I have been with you on numerous occasions when a nurse had trouble finding the right insertion point in the right vein, necessitating multiple attempts. You have never so much as winced, though you have perfected the eye roll that only I could see.

Psychologically, I know you are in a kind of shock about this quick turn of events. It wasn't that long ago when we were sitting at a baseball game, thinking that you only had a cyst in your breast, which would be dissolved, you were sure, with medication. Now you are facing a steady diet of chemo with an extra generous helping of double-mastectomy surgery.

And now your chemo nurse advises you to talk to your surgeon about having a port-a-cath installed in your chest above your heart. This will obviate the need to always infuse the chemo through your arm. Eventually, the veins in your arm will collapse and become useless. The port-a-cath is a permanent onramp to your bloodstream, an artificial connection to your aortic artery. The needle goes into the port-a-cath instead of into your actual vein, saving the vein and speeding up the infusion of the drug into your system, since it is located close to your heart. Another procedure. Another part of the offensive plan, thus, not a setback but another tactic to maintain a positive outlook.

We have learned an awful lot from your chemo nurse, as much as we have learned from your oncologist.

CHAPTER NINE

Like Shopping for Curtains

Your surgeon reflects more life than death in his sparkling eyes. He hails from South Africa, and his manner possesses an exquisite grace and sensitivity that seems calmly reassuring. He speaks softly and directly. No condescension. No patronization. He imparts facts with fluid confidence. Surety. He has been here many times before. His quiet, measured manner says that you will be his patient for a very long time. He knows that we know he cannot say this with words, so he says this with careful gestures and facial expressions.

We discuss briefly the hospital where he will perform the surgery. It is his primary home base. His team is veteran, exceedingly competent, and conscientious to a fault. Your oncologist will determine the date after your first two rounds of chemotherapy. Discharge will be the same day as surgery, unless your recovery is complicated, which it should not be. The anesthesiologists he works with are top-notch; they will see to a smooth recovery.

You will arrive with breasts on the day of surgery early, around 5:00 a.m. The surgeon has taken a liking to you. He wants you to be first on his docket that day. You will be on the operating table for no more than two hours. You will be in recovery for a few hours, till early afternoon at the latest. You will be discharged same day without breasts and assorted nodes, tissue, and muscle; home before dinnertime, though you will not feel much like eating.

Matter-of-factly, he lowers your exam gown and begins drawing on your chest. He indicates where the incisions will be made. The lines run horizontally across both breasts. Your nipples will be sacrificed. Tissue expanders will be inserted. Later, the actual breast implants will replace the expanders. Nipples can be recreated, but it will mean excising more skin and tissue from your lower back. We decline that option. Nipples are only nipples.

The surgeon draws dots under your left arm where the likely lymph nodes will need to be excised. He promises to leave as much tissue and muscle as he thinks prudent.

The left breast is the origin of the cancerous cells. The right breast will be taken as a precautionary measure. This decision is yours, which the surgeon thinks wise.

We are in and out of his exam office as if we had been shopping for curtains.

CHAPTER TEN

Steel Core Required

A *stage 4* breast cancer diagnosis at age forty-four demands a steel core of physical endurance, emotional grace, intellectual resolve, and spiritual surety. Your steel core has always been apparent to me, but never more so than in the face of cancer.

I don't know that it matters what your core can be attributed to, if anything at all, or any combination of things. Maybe it is simply an innate blessing. The nature-versus-nurture debate seems trivial and irrelevant at the moment, but in my attempt to understand more fully who you are and what enables you to thrive while death courts you, I note the following:

Perhaps it is the fact that you grew up with three rugged, athletic brothers (bench-press records, fifty-mile bike rides, Friday-night glories, motorcycles, bloody knuckles, and deer hunting). You were always surrounded and outnumbered, always being tested. This never-ending battle of testosterone against estrogen consumed your formative years and instilled in you toughness and temerity that cancer will have to respect.

Perhaps it is the fact that your childhood was embedded in the patriarchy of midtwentieth-century Indiana. For a female, stiff odds and no easy days. You refused to let society define the expectations you set for yourself. You left your safe but stifling environment at the earliest opportunity, accepting an athletic scholarship to a Texas university and creating an uncharted, expansive new home for yourself. Every day, the battle against cancer demands that you venture in mind and body into uncharted realms, alone. Fortunately, you have a history of doing just that.

Perhaps it is the fact that your southern Indiana childhood was tested by seemingly unending months of overcast skies and dreary mixtures of rain, sleet, and snow, all of which exploited even the mildest tendency to despair. You maintained your positive outlook when so many others withdrew into debilitating introspection, ennui, misplaced anger, and alcoholism.

Perhaps it is the fact that a hurricane, an all-too-present nemesis in the Ohio valley, descended in your sophomore year of high school upon your house with lethal fury. You sought refuge in a bathtub, using a mattress for a shield. The remembered sight of your house minus a roof still shocks your senses some thirty years later. You found a way to survive then, when the enemy was a hurricane, and you are finding a way to survive now, when the enemy is cancer.

Perhaps it is the fact that you escaped the limitations of southern Indiana by earning a tennis scholarship to Southwest Texas State University, the college home of LBJ and George Straight. You embarked upon a path of achievement and independence, balancing all-day practice sessions in merciless Southern humidity with disciplined, lonely study in the library, earning a summa cum laude degree in English in four years.

Perhaps it is the fact that decades later, as a teacher, you taught castaway students, ranging in age from six to fourteen in a one-room schoolhouse in the middle of the Mojave Desert, an outpost of educational civilization. The formal curriculum was the usual array of academic subjects, but your real job was emotional nurturing and character development with students who were at a premature crossroads in life— civilized behavior versus criminality, seasoned with various forms of self- destruction. Your own emotional stability and character willed them against terrible odds to positive life choices. In your classroom, physical education consisted of seven-mile hikes exploring the desert landscape, talking nonstop to socialize and develop your students' language skills, and testing physical and psychological endurance in the face of desert sun, wind, and dust storms. Your students, who were willing to prove their toughness by boxing a freight train, call you years later to let you know they are still trying to heed your teaching, even when they are failing, and to ask about your fight against the evil "C."

Perhaps it is simply your nature that accounts for your ability to stand toe-to-toe with death and trade punches.

CHAPTER ELEVEN

Mother and Son

We know that one side effect of your chemotherapy treatments will be hair loss. Sure enough, within days of your first two chemotherapy sessions, you are combing out swaths of hair. With your fingers and without any force, you are able to pull strands of hair from your scalp as if they were not connected. You are not shocked, but you didn't think your hair would go so quickly. After a day or two of sitting on the couch, combing out hair, you decide to shave your head. Better to get it over with all at once rather than lose hair gradually. You enlist your younger son, Trent, in the shaving. He thinks doing this is a great idea. In fact, he is anxious to see what you look like bald. "Mom, let's do this. You will look better bald than with patches of scalp showing."

You and Trent, your younger son, retreat to the bathroom to do the job. I am shut out. This is a mother-and-son moment. Besides, you trust Trent's skill at shaving your scalp more than mine. You know he will be patient and steady-handed. I tend to move too quickly and carelessly. You want to lose hair, not skin.

I hear both of you laughing and talking nonstop. I stand outside the closed door, admiring and loving you both. Trent is all of ten years old, but he is mature beyond his years. Shaving your head is for him a way to join you in your fight against cancer. Trent is for you an extremely capable soldier.

When the clippers are shut off, I hear Trent's proud voice say, "Mom, you have a beautiful head. It really has a great shape. It's really even and smooth all the way around."

You and Trent exit the bathroom. You are behind him with your arms draped over his shoulders. He looks as proud of his mother as any son possibly could. You are smiling ear to ear. No tears, no self-pity, no regrets. "It feels so much better. Getting ready in the morning will be a piece of cake."

In letting Trent know that you have cancer, we have assured him that you have excellent doctors, and we are confident that your treatment plan will defeat the disease. We have stated with unequivocal certainty that you will be around not only to see him graduate not only from high school but from college as well. We inform him with all the matter-of-factness we can muster that we are determined to carry on with our daily lives, and we will fight cancer as a team and beat it into submission. Trent tells us that we just need to let him know what we need him to do. You look at him with so much love that all I can do is leave the room and hide in the bathroom for a few minutes to regain my composure.

A day arrives when you announce that you want to go shopping for a wig. You have been going out often with your bald head showing, sometimes with a scarf or a baseball cap. A scarf annoys you. When you tie it tightly, you complain that it puts too much pressure on your head. When you tie it loosely, you complain that it slips and you have to constantly readjust it.

We visit a salon in downtown Bakersfield that specializes in wigs. The cutting is done downstairs; the wigs are fitted upstairs. The salesperson is polite and accommodating. You try on multiple wigs in various colors and styles. In your youth, your natural hair color was blond. Over time, your hair darkened, and you maintained the blond with the aid of artificial color. You really don't care about color now. You want something that feels comfortable and will not look ridiculous. After an hour of trying on an assortment of wigs, you leave without a purchase. Every wig felt itchy and restrictive. You laughed at how most of them made you look: unnatural, silly, and in your own words, desperate.

I remind you that many people, friends and strangers alike, have complimented you on your "beautiful baldness." We exit the store celebrating that consolation.

CHAPTER TWELVE

Bilateral Takes on New Meaning

❧

The day of your bilateral mastectomy is upon us. I am pondering the term *bilateral*. Until now, the term has held only a relatively innocuous position in my lexicon. In high school geometry, we examined bilateral triangles. In high school history, we studied bilateral trade agreements and bilateral arms-control negotiations. Otherwise, the term has held no sway.

Now, a doctor is about to remove the most telling features of your torso. A sawing is about to occur. Excavation. Removal. Reconstruction and restoration with tissue expanders and silicone implants. I have never felt so nostalgic about high school geometry and history.

We have lived through surgeries before, but this one is clearly different. You are anxious to go under the knife, to have the doctor cut away everything that threatens survival. For as long as I have known you, life to you was and is something sacred, something you are thankful for each and every day. It remains so as you are wheeled out of pre-op and into surgery.

Your sense of humor astonishes me. You are ready to say goodbye to your breasts that have caused more trouble than they have been worth, as you have wryly noted. You look forward to not having so much strain on your back. You will have more flexibility to swing a tennis racquet. You will be able to purchase a wider variety of blouses, shirts, and dresses. You will be able to run without so much annoying bounce. You will have better posture. As you make these statements, you are smiling and laughing. I am in awe of the equanimity with which you are accepting your cruel fate.

As your gurney rolls toward the double doors that conceal the operating rooms, I am thinking about the irony of your bilateral procedure that will be performed unilaterally on you. I impotently wish I could trade places with you. I illogically wish I could go through the operation with you. I fervently pray that your doctors operate as competently as they have explained their methods and contingencies. I restlessly wait.

You are home, but you are not home. Your body is lying on our sofa, but it is not your body. Your body has been taken from you for a necessary reason, but that reason is now only an abstraction. Your reality is that your body is no longer something that you recognize. It has been altered, which you were prepared for, but you didn't know that it would be so wholly taken from you, seemingly removed to a place beyond your possession. Your eyes are mostly closed, but when they open, it is not you that I see. A vacancy fills your pupils like I have never seen a vacancy take up space before. That is not quite true. I have seen such a vacancy before, in my father's eyes in the days leading to his death. I knew that he could not see me in those final hours. I hope he was seeing God, but I know that he was not seeing me. I'm not even sure I was seeing him. He was already gone before he was gone. You are not gone. I know that you can see me. You are telling me that your chest is on fire. You can feel the tissue expanders doing their work. You can feel your breasts that are no longer part of you. Their absence is palpable. Fire consumes your upper body. The slightest movement intensifies the burning. Your lower body is numb. I put a fresh pair of the hospital socks on your feet, but you can't feel your feet. We brought home several pairs, and you want the yellow ones instead of the white ones. You are not sure if you are home or still in the hospital. I put the TV on for you as distraction, but the fire engulfing your torso is keeping you isolated from any normal input. You can barely hear my voice. Sometimes sound gets through to you, but you are hardly aware of my words. There is no real meaning other than letting you know that I am in the room and not going anywhere unless you need something. That is the only meaning that counts right now. The TV is no distraction for me either. I sit and watch you writhe in unimaginable pain—the pain that comes from the burning, the pain that comes from your breasts that are no longer part of you, and the pain that comes from knowing that you have entered a world from which no return is possible.

Your pain and misery are truly bilateral, encompassing equally your mental and physical realms.

CHAPTER THIRTEEN

Settling In to Misery's Routine

W e have adjusted to the routine of the cancer center's infusion center. How we are adapting to the most unpleasant circumstances is both gratifying and disappointing. We have learned the names of the nurses, where they come from, how long they have been working at the CBCC. We know which ones perform with care, speed, and efficiency and which ones seem emotionally absent, professionally distracted, and generally slow and inattentive. The good ones far outnumber those we think need improvement.

We know which phlebotomists can effortlessly and precisely hit your vein on the first try for your blood draws and which ones are hopelessly and laboriously imprecise, often needing multiple attempts and sometimes seeking help after utter failure. You are most accommodating; you never wince or flinch. If I look upset, you scold me with your eyes.

We have learned to ask for your lab results. Your oncologist, physicians' assistants, and nurses never volunteer to provide them. We are most concerned about your white and red blood cell counts. Chemo notoriously denigrates these counts, sapping your strength and compromising your immune system.

Experientially, the chemo treatments are fairly innocuous. We have quickly learned the patterns of the treatment center. We have our preferred seats in the large waiting room, near the large TV monitor that alternates a cable news channel I like with cooking and home and garden channels that you enjoy. We also like to sit near an oversize aquarium that features exotic and colorful fish species that give us joy while we wait for your name to be called.

We have figured out which of your fellow patients handle their treatments with stoicism and which ones self-indulgently express their suffering through complaining, sighing, moaning, dramatic coughing fits, and fidgeting in their recliners.

We know where the restrooms are and have learned how to navigate the pathways with your IV stand in tow.

The aftermath of the treatments emerges as the real evil. I must accept at face value what the nurses have told us about chemo in the twenty-first century producing less physically traumatic side effects than ever before in its history. I have nothing to use for comparison. I only know the aftermath that you must endure.

We are learning that the first twenty-four hours after a chemo treatment is falsely innocuous. You are tired from the emotional ordeal of the treatment more than you are from the physical experience. Your appetite has been suppressed dramatically, but you have no trouble drinking water. Your body desires rest, but you are reasonably yourself.

The second day emerges as the day of reckoning. The full impact of the chemo treatment hits you like one-hundred-pound sandbags. Your body is reduced to rubble.

To say that exhaustion results from your treatments is to understate in the most profound sense the meaning of that word. Any movement whatsoever requires a gathering of will that itself exhausts your most limited supply of strength. Helping you lift your head to readjust a pillow feels to me like an act of torture. It is as if your limbs are not connected to your body's frame. They are lifeless to the point of shock and disbelief. Your body seems to sink into the bed, sofa, or chair to the point of disappearing.

If you had an appetite, you would be too tired to chew and swallow. As it is, you must force yourself to eat morsels of food, only to have them regurgitated. A visit to the bathroom becomes a journey of extreme exertion. Sitting on and getting up from the toilet requires assistance.

Diarrhea seems to be relieved only by constipation. Balance between these extremes proves quite elusive.

As one who has never consumed any significant amount of alcohol, you were unfamiliar with the pleasantries of vomiting until chemo. Now, you are an expert. I will never get used to seeing you hunched over a trash can, toilet bowl, or sink, but I am getting less shocked by the sight. I know not to get too close to you as to add to the trauma, but to be ready with a glass of water or ginger ale and a wet washcloth.

CHAPTER FOURTEEN

Distractions and Life Not Like the Movies

Several months into your treatment, which has been a combination of chemotherapy, radiation, bilateral mastectomy, insertion of breast implants, and insertion of a port-a-cath, we find ourselves in your oncologist's office for a "state of the treatment" assessment. I have pleaded with you not to shift the focus of your appointment from yourself to your doctor's life. You are expert at avoiding, understandably, a direct discussion of your cancer and its progression through your system. After all, the disease's reputation is lethal. The conventional wisdom suggests that people diagnosed with one of the big four cancers—brain, breast, lung, and organ—usually die, if not from the cancer then from one or a combination of its brutal side effects. Your oncologist has been up front in saying that among the big four, breast is the one that promises the longest survival rate. This has been a comfort to you, however small.

In your attempts to avoid discussing your disease, we have learned that your oncologist, who is from India, maintains a home in his native country and regularly visits his elderly mother, who, despite her advanced age, still lives independently. Aside from wanting to avoid talking about your disease, you are genuinely interested in your oncologist's stories about India. In fact, if your immune system were not so compromised from the chemo, you would like to travel there. He is a most charming man, and his love of his country is obvious.

Your doctor has graciously responded to all your questions about India, perhaps as happy to discuss a subject other than cancer as you are. He has made us laugh on more than one occasion, as he has shared stories of his trips to visit his mother. In your doctor's opinion, the summer heat of India makes Bakersfield's heat seem mild by comparison, and the effects of the heat are exacerbated by the lack of widespread air- conditioning that we are spoiled by. In your doctor's opinion, driving in India for a visitor is suicidal. The roads are filled with all sorts of people, wildlife, and modes of transportation. Rules of the road are nothing more than theoretical abstracts. Your doctor always hires a driver who possesses the temperament and skill to navigate vehicles, bicycles, scooters, farm equipment, manic taxi drivers, goats, dogs, cows, elephants, pedestrians, buses, and human-powered rickshaws.

We have also laughed freely as your doctor has described how India's dense population complicates all facets of living. He becomes particularly frustrated when he visits museums, something he loves, and must endure parades of people who squeeze between his stance in front of a piece of artwork and the artwork itself, however small a gap he leaves. Apparently, people in India do not share the typical American's sense of inviolable space.

Your oncologist has also made us feel eternally grateful that we live in America and that you are being treated here for cancer rather than in his home country. According to your doctor, in India, doctors refrain from exploring all possible treatment options, especially for the elderly. We had shared with your doctor my father's health issues and the aggressive medical treatment he is benefitting from in his ninth decade. These issues include heart attack, severe diverticulitis, extensive arthritis, debilitating hearing loss, and hardening of the arteries. As a doctor in India, he would be expected to send my father home without much treatment to expire gradually and passively. We are immensely thankful that your doctor believes in and practices aggressive medical care, regardless of one's age or condition. We are confident that your doctor will explore every possible treatment to keep you alive and to maximize your quality of life.

I sometimes feel exasperated as you steer the conversation away from your health status and toward the doctor's life. I understand why you do this and love you for your genuine interest in other people's lives. You are a naturally curious and gregarious person, and talking about yourself makes you uncomfortable. You also understandably exhibit trepidation about discovering just how dire your situation may be. I am also frustrated that we sometimes squander the precious time we have in our infrequent visits with your oncologist.

But in this particular consultation, you have sat down on the exam table with a purpose, other than to listen to stories about India. You want to know, like Lou Gehrig in *Pride of the Yankees*, "if it's three strikes, Doc?"

Of course, you know well that your inquiry must be circumspect. Your doctor has been carefully measured in every statement he has made about your condition and treatment. He has made it clear that no one knows exactly how a patient will respond to various chemotherapy concoctions. That is what makes effective cancer treatment so elusive. There are so many forms of breast cancer, and thus so many specific drugs, dosages, and targeting strategies.

Your doctor has also made it clear that he believes in God and the power of divine intervention. He has encouraged you more than once to pray as part of your treatment. That has been a message that you have appreciated as well-intentioned, albeit gratuitous. You have always been a deeply spiritual person who makes prayer a daily part of her life, before cancer and certainly with cancer.

So it was with extreme sensitivity and tact that you made the most important inquiry of your life. "Doctor, have you ever had any patients who are in a similar circumstance as I am in terms of age, disease, and treatment?" The doctor's response was in the affirmative. You continued, "So what is the longest length of time that they have survived?"

I could sense your doctor was growing more than a bit uncomfortable. He uncrossed and recrossed his legs and adjusted his glasses, which tended to slide down his nose. I give him credit for maintaining eye contact with you, however, which I felt validated his veracity. During this long pause before he began to speak, he nodded his head up and down in obvious reflection. "I have a patient who has lived for nine years. That is the longest period of survival."

We were both surprised at how specific your doctor's response turned out to be. For both of us, the number nine immediately took on a garish and sobering aura. We left the office feeling gratified that we got a direct answer to your inquiry, and also questioning whether the answer we got was something we could live with.

Not surprisingly, the bravado displayed in movies proves hard to duplicate in real life.

CHAPTER FIFTEEN

Cold, Hard Number 9

We spend a few days contemplating the implications of your doctor's statement that the longest time one of his patients, similar to you in age and disease circumstances, had survived was nine years. In answering your question, your doctor had emphasized the words *nine years* by lowering his voice. He was normally soft-spoken, and he had intentionally softened his voice even more as a way to sound hopeful and encouraging.

The first unpleasant implication was that the patient he referred to was the exception, not the rule. If you were similarly exceptional, that would get you to age fifty-three. The second implication was that a death within the nine-year period was a distinct possibility. This was clearly something that you already knew, but hearing the cancer expert implying this out loud was staggering in its effect. Your doctor meant to be encouraging in giving you a direct answer to your question. His personal and professional integrity would not allow him to minimize the daunting challenge you were facing.

The words *nine years* reverberated in our minds as a kind of demarcation line—an outpost reserved especially for you, a cloud that insistently appeared on any horizon real or imagined. We tried, each in our own way, to exert a sense of will to defy the external force of your doctor's answer. At times, we mocked the nine-year example: "So, what does this have to do with me? I'm a wholly different person with a different outlook and different constitution." At other times, we considered that treatments and drugs, particularly for breast cancer patients, were constantly improving.

Your competitive nature accepted the nine-year example as a kind of challenge. In your mind, your oncologist had thrown down a gauntlet and dared you to surpass it.

You quickly placed the number 53 in the context of our sons' ages. When you turned fifty-three, our oldest son would be twenty-eight. Our youngest son would be nineteen. Seeing our sons through to these ages became an aspect of the gauntlet that you immediately accepted and became all the more determined to overcome. Our oldest would be well into adulthood with college completed and, hopefully, a career started. Our youngest would be through high school and hopefully into college and on his way to a degree. The number 53 would never lose its sting, but the pain diminished slightly as you contemplated where our sons would probably be on their life paths.

Thinking about average life expectancies in this modern age causes one to feel a sense of entitlement, however irrational that may be, which you now had to rationally reconsider. You bravely did exactly that. I, on the other hand, sought refuge in the persona of the "never say die" coach, willing his athlete to victory against seemingly insurmountable odds. Not for the first time did you tell me that I needed to pull myself out of foolhardy denial.

CHAPTER SIXTEEN

To Nipple or Not to Nipple

To say that American culture is fascinated by and even obsessed with the female breast may be an understatement of epic proportions. So much of women's fashion is designed to accentuate and show off breasts. By under- and overgarments, breasts are lifted, squeezed, enhanced, enlarged, shadowed, teased, and sometimes revealed. Breast measurements, in inches and cup sizes, are routinely mentioned in descriptions of actresses and models. The word *rack* usually has one dominant connotation that makes using the word in a different context problematic. The clothing enterprise *Victoria's Secret* has seemingly been built on breast adornment. Acclaimed novelist Philip Roth explored our culture's breast obsession by writing a novel, entitled *The Breast*, about a man who wakes up as a female breast.

Female nipples are equally fascinating in our culture. The TV show *Seinfeld* has an entire episode revolving around one of the character Elaine's nipples, inadvertently photographed by the character Kramer and revealed in a Christmas card photo. In our media, articles about actresses, singers, and other celebrities often refer to intentional or accidental "nip slips."

It is in this context that you, a forty-three-year-old woman, must answer the question posed by your breast reconstruction surgeon: "Do you want nipples?" To our ears, his question rings absurd but understandable. As a male, I have no way of knowing how this question threatens your femininity. You have already had your breasts removed; skin expanders were inserted in preparation for implants. Perhaps you had already redefined in your own mind traditional notions of femininity, and the doctor's question about nipples struck you simply as ridiculous.

In response to the question, you smile shyly and ask how exactly nipples can be created. Your surgeon explains that he will have to excise skin from your lower back or thighs and then form the skin into a facsimile of a nipple. Twice. The consequence will be lifelong sensitivity in the area sacrificing the skin. Wearing clothes, leaning against a chairback, or sliding into a restaurant booth will forever create discomfort and pain.

All in the name of nipples.

In order to help you make a decision, the doctor offers to show us pictures of what a manufactured nipple looks like. You glance at me, and I know exactly what you are thinking. I am thinking the same thing. In the context of cancer, nipples are wholly irrelevant. You have been through so many procedures that the thought of more surgery to remove skin and tissue from a part of your body that is without disease seems nonsensical. Your doctor reads our nonverbal communication and concludes that you will be comfortable without nipples. That you have escaped one more surgical procedure clearly registers as relief on your face.

Nipples are just nipples; cancer is not just cancer. Cancer is your madly tenacious enemy, and you don't have time to be distracted or worn down by meaningless moves.

CHAPTER SEVENTEEN

Nipple Transplants and Trading Places

❧

D riving home from your decision to forego nipples, I try to make you laugh by offering to give you my nipples, since I've never had much use for them or done much with them. Without false modesty, I confess that my nipples would serve as a poor substitute for yours, but under the circumstances, they are all I have to offer.

After we laugh a bit, I try to convince you that my offer is real. You dismiss it as absurd and then say that there is something a little creepy about a nipple transplant. I resist an urge to continue discussing the possibility, as you just want to get home.

In my mind, I wonder about a national nipple registry of donors. I also absurdly ponder whether nipples are gender-specific or androgynous. I refrain from sharing these thoughts with you.

After an interval of silence, I tell you that I would gladly trade places with you. I tell you that I have asked God to remove the cancer from your body and place it in mine. When you look at me as if I'm crazy, I tell you that you deserve to be alive and disease-free much more than I do. My evidence is that you are a better person all around and one who appreciates life and loves life so much more than I do.

I also tell you that I want to repay you for saving me with your love from a meaningless life by saving you from cancer. You adamantly respond that you would never ask me to do that or want me to do that or accept me doing that. I tell you gently that I will still pray that somehow we can trade places.

You end the discussion by telling me that you need to rest and I need to concentrate on my driving. All you want is to go home.

CHAPTER EIGHTEEN

Mother and Son

You talk on the phone with your older son, John-Michael. He is living in Ventura, attending community college, living with friends in a cramped apartment five minutes from the beach, delivering pizza to make rent and pocket change.

John-Michael is establishing independence, learning about the world, sowing oats, figuring out what kind of stakes he wants to set down and where.

You are so proud that he is finding a footing in the world. You want to protect and preserve all the youthful delight he can experience in these tender but less-innocent years. You want to insulate him from your cancer, from its effects on you and on how you interact with the world. At the same time, you know you must answer the tolling bell in your conscience: the mother John-Michael has always known is forever being changed by a random, angry enemy, and your existence is being threatened as never before. You talk in hushed tones, your voice barely audible to me as I sit next to you on the sofa, holding your hand. Cancer has pushed the years of raised voices and minor and major conflicts far into the past. You wisely know that you must begin conversations with John-Michael that anticipate his needs and questions years into the future. You must reassure him with quiet confidence as you struggle in ever-increasing desperation to reassure yourself. You must utter words that will resonate in his consciousness when he will be responsible for knowing when you may not be able or around to remind him of his knowing. You seek words and tones to hide your struggle as you also prepare him today for far less youthful, less joyful, and less innocent tomorrows.

CHAPTER NINETEEN

A Teacher and Lover of Students

W hen you were first diagnosed with *stage 4* cancer, I refused to accept the fact that *stage 4* meant terminal. You accepted this truth, but I refused to. From the very outset of your battle with the disease, I have preached victory and have never for a moment accepted the possibility of defeat.

To your credit, you have never once adopted a self-pitying persona in order to convince me that I was in denial. You have stoically refrained from descending into a woe-is-me attitude. Instead, you have urged me to prepare myself for the most likely eventuality: premature death due to cancer or a cancer-related illness or condition. You have done this in the most understated, nondramatic, prosaic manner possible. I am in awe of your self-composure and grace.

Under no circumstances would I be able to handle your situation with anything close to your maturity and calm composure. Even without the gun barrel of cancer pressing against my skull, I tend toward a negative outlook where my own life is concerned.

Learning to fight against this tendency has been a lifelong struggle. Were I in your situation, I fear that I would all too quickly adopt the persona of a drama queen. I would be hopelessly self-pitying and all too willing to play the role of martyr.

Despite my tendency to be negative about myself, where others are concerned, I am eternally hopeful. In looking at your cancer with unbridled optimism, I also have felt in my heart that if anyone could disprove the certainty of a stage 4 diagnosis, you could. That stands as a testament to how much faith I have always had in your mental, emotional, spiritual, and physical toughness. My greatest faith has always been in the power of your indomitable spirit to win out over overwhelming odds and realities.

You have exceeded all reasonable expectations of how you would respond to a cancer diagnosis and rigorous, debilitating treatment. During the first year and a half of your battle, you continued working as an elementary school teacher. I am in awe of your ability to undergo chemotherapy and somehow gather your shattered strength and overcome a suppressed immune system to teach.

The first year of your battle, you were teaching kindergartners. As a high school teacher, I underappreciated the challenges that surface in a kindergarten class. In supporting your efforts to continue working, I had ample opportunity to develop a sincere appreciation for what you faced.

Together, we would go to your school on Saturdays and Sundays to help you prepare for the upcoming week of instruction. As a perfectionist about the learning environment you created for your students, you insisted that we spend hours upon hours getting your classroom ready. Every bulletin board played an integral part of your instruction. Decorations were not simply decorations; they were instructional tools to enhance your students' academic development. Your bulletin boards were artistic and thematic. One of them showed beautifully drawn fish of myriad colors swimming in an ocean with waves rippling. You were encouraging students to learn to navigate their way through school challenges. You were also encouraging students to rise to the top of your class through appropriate behavior, effort, and exemplary academic performance. You changed bulletin boards multiple times throughout the school year to suit your curriculum. Your bulletin boards helped students learn the days of the week, the months of the year, decimal places, verb tenses, and other learning targets. Your boards celebrated historical figures and national holidays in marvelous displays of artwork, vibrant colors, and valuable vocabulary. You turned a word wall into a work of art.

We fired up the duplication machines to make sure you had sufficient materials. This was necessary since your classroom texts were inadequate in content and supply. We copied, we collated, we stacked, we hauled, and we distributed.

I learned the intricacies of the Ellison machine, which professionally cuts letters from construction paper. Cancer or no cancer, you were intent on creating bulletin boards that were works of art, aesthetically pleasing, as well as academically valuable.

I have no idea how you managed to give each of your students the personal attention he or she desperately needed while undergoing exhausting chemo treatments. I also have no idea how you maintained your sense of humor with your students, when all your spare energy was needed to recover from chemo. As an example, you teasingly referred to one student named Ernie as Bert, playing off the famous *Sesame Street* characters. By the end of the school year, you were calling him Bernie, combining both names. I loved hearing your stories about how Ernie would roll his eyes at your gentle teasing, teasing you back by pretending to be highly offended while actually loving the attention. You had another student whose last name was Easter. Of course, you called him every other holiday under the sun, including Christmas, Fourth of July, Memorial Day, and so on. This student also never refrained from raising his hand in class not just to answer a question but also to see what holiday you would substitute for his real name.

You work with a population of black, white, and Latino students who came from impoverished socioeconomic backgrounds. Some of the parents were involved in criminal behavior involving gangs or drugs or both. Some of the parents had been or were currently incarcerated. These students were the recipients of your excellent teaching and, more importantly, of your caring personal attention and efforts to motivate them to effect generational change in their lives. Numerous students maintain contact with you through phone calls and texting to keep you updated on their lives. One young man is currently attending Howard University; when he returns home, you take him out to lunch and on shopping trips for clothes.

Not for a moment have you allowed negativity or cynicism to invade your love for students and teaching. Many of them only learned about your cancer when you lost your hair due to chemo. Otherwise, they might have never known from your words, demeanor, untamed enthusiasm, unflinching sense of humor, and spirited dedication to their learning.

CHAPTER TWENTY

One Year In

During your first year of battling cancer, you have withstood six chemotherapy treatments. Each successive session has exhausted you more than the last one. Somehow, you have continued to work as a kindergarten teacher, refusing to give up your career out of your sense of optimism, loyalty, and commitment.

Your school district, Mojave Unified in Mojave, California, has been enormously supportive, from your principal to the custodians to the district office personnel. Your teaching colleagues have shown themselves to be wonderfully empathic, sensitive, and bolstering. They have treated you with what Bruce Springsteen sings about in his song "Human Touch." Your colleagues have given you the most loving and tender human touching imaginable. They check on you in your classroom, they offer to complete everyday tasks for you, they chat with you when they sense that you cannot be alone for fear of an emotional collapse, they donate days and days of their own accrued sick leave so you can take all the time you need to get treatment without sacrificing your income, they place you on their respective churches' prayer lists, and they include you in their own private prayers.

You miss school days, of course, for your chemo treatments, which consume at least half a day for the actual treatment and two additional hours for travel time. You sometimes miss a day or two after the treatment, though usually not the first posttreatment day.

The second and third days are far more debilitating, when the drugs are fully infused in your system and searching for and destroying cancer cells.

Your oncologist has suggested that you keep working for as long as you feel you are able to. He has advised you to take special care to avoid picking up germs from your students, which is virtually impossible. It is well known that chemo suppresses one's immune system, and classroom teachers are especially vulnerable to contagious illnesses. Kindergarten teachers also have to deal with runny noses and bathroom issues as a matter of routine. Hand sanitizer has become one of your best friends. But you are determined to continue living your life, and that involves teaching.

Radiation treatments were administered shortly after your sixth chemo session. This strategy intended to prevent the cancer from spreading. Your oncologist made it clear that at all costs, we needed to keep cancer out of your lungs, organs, and brain. We viewed radiation as another form of heavy artillery in your war. Despite feeling exhausted to the point of utter physical collapse, you were maintaining a full-speed- ahead attitude. You had adjusted to life without hair, and you were managing bouts of constipation and diarrhea with humor and aplomb. Your students were celebrating having a bald teacher. They collectively thought of it as cool and distinctive. When you showed up to your classroom with a baseball cap on, they urged you to take it off so they could admire the smooth contours of your bald head. For them, having a teacher with hair had become "uncool."

Compared to chemo, radiation is a cakewalk—quick, painless, and comparatively free of side effects. You did suffer from minor skin irritation at the site below your left armpit where the radiation was precisely aimed, but this was mild and hardly worth mentioning compared to vomiting, constipation, diarrhea, nausea, extreme fatigue, loss of appetite, and hair loss. The most noteworthy problem with your radiation treatments was the fact that you had to travel one hour to Bakersfield every day for a period of a few weeks to get radiated. The drive rather than the treatment became tiresome. As usual, you quickly developed an easygoing rapport with your radiologist and his staff of nurses, and you turned the treatments into pleasant social interactions. Again, the medical and support staff of the CBCC proved to be kind, caring, attentive, and exceedingly professional.

The first person to raise the issue of you having a port-a-cath inserted into your chest is one of your chemotherapy nurses. She mentions this during your second chemo treatment. She explains that a port-a-cath is a device that makes it easier to administer chemo and draw your blood for analysis, and that it obviates the risk of overusing the veins in your arm to the point of possible collapse. You are intrigued at this suggestion, especially because nurses sometimes struggle to access the right vein in your arm for your frequent blood work.

As the nurse sets you up for your chemo session, she points out a few patients in the infusion center who are having their chemo delivered through their chest rather than an arm. The port-a-cath is surgically placed a few inches beneath the collarbone, to one side or the other. The port is about the size of a quarter and sits just under the skin. The catheter is a tube that connects to the jugular vein, which runs down to the heart. The nurse convinces us that a port-a-cath will be a much healthier and efficient way to experience chemotherapy.

The doctor we see about having your port-a-cath installed is the same one who performed your bilateral mastectomy. He further convinces us that this will prove to be a good decision. He explains that chemo drugs are so toxic that over time, they can cause serious irritation to the skin and your veins. Eventually, veins in your arm can become scarred and blocked, rendering the vein useless. Having chemo infused into the much larger jugular vein allows the toxic drugs to be immediately diluted by a greater volume of blood, thus reducing the risk of damage to the vein itself as well as skin and surrounding tissue.

The doctor seals the deal by telling us that the procedure to insert the port-a-cath is done on an outpatient basis. He can get on and off the operating table in less than an hour, and your chemo treatments and blood draws will be much less painful and much more efficient and healthy. You are scheduled to have one more procedure, thankfully minor, with major benefits.

The port-a-cath appears to me like a thimble beneath the surface of your skin. You have a two-inch scar running parallel to your clavicle just above the device. We apply vitamin E nightly to heal the incision's redness. The veins in your arm are happy.

At home we talk quietly about the myriad challenges that have you in the crosshairs. You have little time to prepare yourself for one trial before another one pops up. You have had to endure the initial blow of the cancer diagnosis. You were deprived of at least starting your fight as a stage 1 patient; instead, you were given a stage 4 prognosis, meaning your treatment from the outset was defined as palliative. That term signifies no cure, only a delay of the inevitable end of life. You have had to reconcile that harsh reality and formulate a positive outlook in order to live day to day, to continue interacting with the world, and to increase the efficacy of your treatments. We have taken that medical diagnosis of care without cure and embedded it in a context of faith in God, faith in the powers of your enormously positive attitude, and faith in the power of prayer. Your body has been stripped of breasts, replaced by tissue expanders and silicone implants. You are being radiated. Your chest has now been outfitted with a catheter that feeds into your jugular vein. The chemotherapy drugs are your best hope for delaying cancer's aggressive nature to spread, but you are well aware of the price you will pay for chemo's rampant toxicity. Healthy cells are sacrificed as cancer cells are killed.

You are somehow withstanding the deluge of bad news and unrelenting challenges.

We hold each other like we have never held each other before. Our eyes say words that we cannot allow past our lips.

CHAPTER TWENTY-ONE

Tennis

Agains your doctor's recommendation, you continued to play tennis throughout your second round of chemotherapy. You knew that your bones were losing density and strength as a direct result of the chemo, but you were determined to stay as active as possible for as long as possible. Playing tennis remained one of your great loves in life.

Your doctor preferred walking to tennis. You were amenable to walking, but it was certainly not an activity that you loved. We walked often, between a mile and two miles at a time. You preferred a dirt field for your walking, which your doctor liked also. Cement and asphalt had become a fearsome enemy of your weakening bones. You grew to enjoy walking and enthusiastically added an extra mile on most of our outings. Knowing the benefits of oxygenating your cells and muscles helped us both feel we were beating back cancer's advance.

Your oncologist expressed concern about the likelihood of fractures in the event of a fall on the unforgiving cement of a tennis court. We both knew of relatives and friends who, while fighting a major medical condition, experienced a hastening of death due to a fall and fracture. Defiantly, you simply were unwilling to give up tennis. You weighed the risks and rewards and decided to keep playing.

Our son, Trent, exhilarated your heart by deciding to play, in addition to soccer, tennis for his high school team. Practicing ground strokes with him and watching his slow and steady development filled your heart with immeasurable joy. On the court, you had opportunities to share with Trent your experiences playing high school and college tennis. Trent delighted in your stories as he learned proper footwork, stroke form, and strategy.

I loved seeing our son stare in awe at one of your surefire, whipping ground strokes. Nothing like a strapping teenager well past six feet tall, arms and legs sinewy and fluid, caught flat-footed by a forty-six-year-old mother with cancer as a playing partner. Your face pricelessly displayed disbelief of your own prowess and pride all at once.

Our local tennis courts, located a quarter mile from our home, sits in a bowl surrounded by lush oak trees and peaks exceeding six thousand feet. The courts are neatly isolated, proffering a perfect escape from daily disappointments and frustrations. Some nights we are entertained by a family of raccoons that descend from an oak tree to commence a nightly raid for food. Herds of deer are commonplace. For a while, a hawk seemed annoyed with us that we had invaded its territory. It would dramatically swoop down from a corner light fixture in a show of displeasure, crisscrossing the court above our heads, within reach of lob shots. The first time the hawk objected to our presence, we were startled and even a bit frightened. Afterward, we watched its movements with joy, anticipated its elegant flights of protest, and caught our breath until it returned to its light pole perch.

Your strategy to minimize the risk of falling is to remain fixed at the center of the backline, moving only a few feet in either direction. You become a spectator on any shots in the corners or dink shots barely over the net. We try to hot our shots center court to give you the opportunity to return. For two years, your forehand and backhand shots are remarkably formidable and give us all we could handle, often rendering our returns feeble or complete misses. The smiles you display in these moments of domination radiate an enhanced glow to your end of the court.

Trent's game is steadily growing in power, strategy, and consistency. In appearance and movement, Trent reminds both of us of Stan Smith, the tall tennis pro from the '60s, '70s, and '80s who battled players such as Arthur Ashe, John Newcombe, and John McEnroe. You and I delight in Trent's increasing ability. We take special pleasure in his powerful serves. Though unpredictable and often sailing long or wide, when his serves land in the service court, they are for me nearly impossible to return. With your years of experience playing tennis in college, you are much more used to stinging serves than I am. You are able to return Trent's best serves, but it stretches your talent, which only deepens your pride in him.

On one of our glorious nights of family tennis, a moment arrived which I knew would inevitably arrive but which I labored hard beyond logic to deny. From your usual position at the center of the baseline, your shots began to lack their normal sting and hard bounce. They floated a bit, uncharacteristic air beneath them; I could see the seams of the ball too clearly. Your returns found the court, but they took longer to arrive.

This change was perhaps unnoticed by Trent, as he was intent on improving his game each time out. He had high school matches under his belt and introspectively sought gains with every stroke. My game was essentially to be a backstop and occasionally to attempt a corner shot to assert sadly and unconvincingly that I could compete with you. So I watched you as much as I watched the ball. I will never know if you were aware that your shots were fading in power, but again, I fooled myself. Of course, you had to know. In yet another example of your fierce grace under cancer's relentless assault, you repelled any urge to admit defeat, to indulge in self-pity, or to invite sympathy.

You gave us such a gift on those tennis courts. You defied your doctor's orders to stay off cement surfaces. You loved playing tennis, but more than that, you wanted to participate in Trent's growing tennis prowess. You helped him by example and by instruction; you watched him learn and love the game as you had learned and loved it.

You allowed us to share in your love of the game, to witness what a marvelous player you always were, and to remember how bravely and ferociously you fought cancer's advance.

CHAPTER TWENTY-TWO

Cancer Stays on the Move

I don't know what we were thinking. I guess we thought that after a year of fighting cancer, you would have earned a reprieve. Maybe we even believed you had a chance of beating the disease and your oncologist would declare that you were in remission.

Whatever our thoughts, we had to come to terms with the reality that your cancer had retained its hyperaggressive nature through your surgery, chemo, and radiation. Your oncologist had called a halt to your chemo treatments, knowing that you needed time to recover physically and emotionally from such intense toxicity.

At that time, I failed to read his approach to your treatment, but in retrospect, I understand. Your doctor stopped your chemo treatments to give you an interlude of life with some degree of quality, as life during chemo offers precious little. He also wanted to see how soon the cancer would resume spreading. In our consultations, he said none of what I just described. Instead, he told us he was pleased at how you were responding to the treatment. You were holding up well; your cancer markers were down to a satisfactory level. He ordered a stop to the chemo and continued you on an estrogen-blocker drug and a bone- strengthening drug. I suppose he knew that it was only a matter of time when you would have to start a new round of chemotherapy, although he spared us that truth. He wanted you to invest yourself in your life rather than spend all your time and energy recovering from chemo.

I was fooled by how well you looked. So many people remarked that they found it hard to believe that you even had cancer, except for your hair loss. Your body looked strong, your eyes were bright, and your relative youthfulness still screamed vibrancy and strength.

Of course, these people never saw you laid out corpse-like after a chemo treatment, barely able to adjust your position in bed. They did not see you vomiting after a few bites of food. They did not see you trying desperately to have a bowel movement for several days, only to then contend with diarrhea for hours. They did not witness your ongoing nausea, causing major discomfort when food was within sight or smell. They were not present in the middle of the night when you sat with unblinking eyes, facing death, knowing the grim reaper had selected you and was showing no signs of backing down.

CHAPTER TWENTY-THREE

Expected Setbacks, Unexpected Gifts

You know what your oncologist will tell you before he says a word. You have had a few months' interruption in your chemo treatments, and now we are in consultation to discover whether your most recent body scans show cancer in retreat or on the move.

Having scans every three months proves to be torturous in so many ways. In the days leading up to and especially on the eve of having the scans done, you must come to terms with what the tests might show—that cancer cells are multiplying and spreading indiscriminately. As the technicians are looking at the monitors during the scans, you try to read their eye movements, facial expressions, and body language, as they cannot reveal to you in words what the monitors are showing. Afterward, in the car on the way home, you try to interpret all the technicians' nonverbal behavior. You cannot stop yourself from doing this, even though you are well aware that it is a no-win game destined to increase your fear that your cancer is spreading. On the day of your consultation with your oncologist, you are understandably beside yourself with dread. Tom Petty is right in so many ways: "Waiting is the hardest part."

And you know before you know. More chemo will be necessary as the cancer's aggressive nature sustains.

I could not be more proud of how you receive the news. You display a "whatever it takes" attitude.

In the car on the way home, you fight back tears. You tell me that your teaching colleagues in your school district have offered to donate sick leave to you so you can manage missing school for treatment while holding on to your job. You never asked anyone to do that. They offered; they organized. They got the word out. The days of leave accumulate in startling numbers. These gestures of love and support, in some cases by people that you don't really even know, touch your soul.

CHAPTER TWENTY-FOUR

Goodbye to Teaching

A day that we knew would arrive finally does. You must give up your job as a second-grade teacher. You cannot continue to balance chemotherapy and work. You are missing too many days with your students. Your immune system has been so compromised that you can no longer expose yourself to the germs and illnesses that are ever present in a classroom filled with thirty-six second graders.

Severe pain in your shoulders, hips, and generally throughout your muscles and joints has made it extraordinarily difficult for you to stand before your students and teach or move around the classroom, giving much-needed individual attention. Kneeling or squatting beside a student's desk to offer help or answer questions has become impossibly difficult. You lack the physical strength and stamina to escort your students to the cafeteria and playground for recess and lunch. You are having trouble bending, lifting, and carrying books and other instructional materials. You can no longer maneuver up and down a ladder to put up and take down elaborate bulletin board designs.

When we are home together, you joke about "chemo brain." You have lapses in memory or periods when you seem disengaged from the present. You joke but it is not really funny. Your ability to concentrate and your short-term memory have in reality been compromised. You are also experiencing periods of dizziness. Even when you are not feeling dizzy, your balance is no longer trustworthy. You must brace yourself on counters, furniture, and me when I am with you.

The bottom line is that you feel you can no longer provide a safe learning environment for your students. You no longer have the strength to interact with your students and colleagues as your sense of professionalism commands you to. We begin the process of applying for a medical disability.

The universe never seems to pass up a chance to slap us with bitter irony. When we are healthy, we typically experience days when all we want to do is refrain from going to work. Instead, we push ourselves into the shower and into our vehicle and force ourselves to make it to our job. When we have lost our health and we are sadly exiled to our home, unable to go to work with common reluctance, all we long to do is jump in the shower and then into our vehicle and drive to our job. We long for the "normal" day, with routine frustrations, exhaustion, and complaint. Our exception from the unexceptional stings to our core.

CHAPTER TWENTY-FIVE

What Is Cancer Good For?

- Overcoming one's fear of needles
- Discovering what one looks like bald
- Having strangers in grocery stores and other public places approach with a comprehension of one's plight to ask permission if they can place you on their church's prayer list
- Focusing the mind on only what truly matters
- Developing perspective: understanding that what used to seem like major problems, postcancer, have become minor nuisances, worthless of mention or more than fleeting attention
- Confirming one's belief in God
- Becoming reacquainted with daily prayer
- Being grateful for pain-free interludes, however brief
- Being thankful for the countless seemingly insignificant moments in life, which have now become monumentally important
- Growing closer to the ones you love
- Realizing closeness is bittersweet; sometimes the closeness threatens to destroy one's composure and must be cut off, as physical touch and emotional connection sometimes initiate a flood of tears
- Learning how to sleep sitting up and standing up
- Developing a superhuman tolerance for pain

○ Taking nonsense in stride
○ Jettisoning the pathetic act of complaining
○ Learning how to live while waiting for the phone inevitably to ring
○ Keeping only essential possessions of emotional value
○ Learning how to love unconditionally
○ Learning how to hold on
○ Learning how to let go

CHAPTER TWENTY-SIX

You Fight to Fight Some More

Y ou lie in bed, but instead of sleeping peacefully, you are fighting for your life. We have plenty of evidence that cancer is spreading unimpeded through your body. It is in your tissue, your lymph nodes, your bones, your bone marrow, your lungs, and your liver. But I don't need scans to tell me any of that. I know it when I look into your eyes. I know it when I see you struggle on your feet to the bathroom. I know it when I see you stare off at what I hope is a vision of God, or at least his manifestation as a green field of gentle grass and soft, warm wind. I know it when I see your legs flexing and twitching. I know it when I see your hands gesturing to indicate you are not finished fighting. I know it when I see you lift your head off the pillow to look around the room to remember what you know you must say goodbye to.

I want somehow to honor your courageous fight—to honor the pure integrity of your essential being. I want desperately to acknowledge you as the least confrontational and most loving person I have ever known. You have been and continue to be so unafraid in your fight, so unselfpitying, so unselfish, so willing to engage in battle when it would have been so understandable and easy for you to withdraw from the unrelenting enemy that is cancer and quietly proclaim, "Enough." But you, the least confrontational being, have religiously and relentlessly confronted your disease with your unimaginably deep reservoir of will and strength and sheer guts.

You confront your disease awake, and you confront your disease asleep. And I sit beside you, trying in my feeble way to honor all the fight that you have already waged and all the fight that you are still bravely waging.

A measure of your integrity as a cancer patient is your determination to refrain from becoming addicted to any of the various pain medications your doctors have prescribed. The strongest of these, morphine, scares you so much that you sometimes choose not to take it when you need it most out of a fear that you will become an addict. We talk about the elderly character Mrs. Dubose in Harper Lee's classic novel *To Kill a Mockingbird*. In the final days of that character's terminal disease, Mrs. Dubose courageously weaned herself off morphine, as she wanted to face God "drug-free." You have lived your life completely free of drugs and alcohol, as both were anathema to your very soul. Countless times, I watched you deny yourself a tablet of morphine as a precaution against addiction. I will ponder and respect your integrity and courage for the rest of my life.

CHAPTER TWENTY-SEVEN

Cancer Never Sleeps

A rendering of the changes cancer has wrought in your life will forever remain woefully underestimated. But my need to describe and explain cancer's effects on every aspect of your life compels me nonetheless.

Cancer emerges as a lethal enemy from the shadow of theory to garish light of certainty, from false hope that the evidence of cancer's existence will remain hidden to the exposure of bitter truth nakedly admitted and confessed, from endless possibility to ramrod reality, from escapist fiction to iron-trap fact.

Cancer cannot be sidestepped. It cannot be charmed. It cannot be debated.

Cancer is a choke hold. It is a wrestler's pin to a suffocating mat. Cancer ticks seconds off the game clock, denying sufficient time for a comeback by its victim.

Cancer constricts like a straitjacket laced with razor blades. It pummels like a sledgehammer to one's forehead.

You have been robbed of so much. In the time required to say "You have cancer," a theft occurred of astronomical, unfathomable proportions. Your body has been invaded, but so has every waking thought. The invasion extends to every impulse to embrace life freely without imminent threat, without all senses saturated in dread and doom. The invasion has enveloped every breath, every blink, and every swallow.

Cancer, your sworn enemy, never sleeps. Your enemy never takes a day off. Never goes on vacation. Never gets drunk. Never pretends. Never plays. Never forgets its mission. Consequently, you have been robbed of the luxury of sleep, and peaceful wakefulness has been stripped forever from your grasp.

Before cancer, sleep for you rarely came easily. I used to think of you as a child reluctant to submerge into a swimming pool. You would put off the shock of losing yourself into another state until the last possible moment. For you, sleep was a last-in, last-out proposition.

Eventually, your daily and nightly tasks completed and your mind at ease, you surrendered to sleep as a child welcomes the enticingly warm bathwaters only after excreting all the reluctance and hesitation from his system in fits of objection and movement.

We used to laugh at how often I would be getting up to start my day just as you were crawling into bed, your unwillingness to quit on the day finally overwhelmed by fatigue.

For you, doing laundry or starting a work project would often begin at ten or eleven at night. You said it was your most productive time. The end of evening when most of the world was closing down through the darkest hours of early morning served as your prime time to open up stores of hyperactivity and productivity. Enveloped in darkness, you felt a boundlessness that daylight seemed to close off. Accomplishment had no limits for you while I typically slept, oblivious to your wee-hours mania. I would wake in astonishment to mounds of clean laundry, freshly scrubbed floors, a rearranged garage, newly painted walls, paid bills, income tax records precisely organized, and piles of completed work papers.

But once ready to rest, you would give yourself over to sleep with deep devotion. You let it take you fully. However long you slept, you left it with the same reluctance that you succumbed to it. Waking from your long-delayed deep slumber seemed to violate your very being. Your inner child never exited the sleep's bath easily or willingly. You awoke in slow motion, delaying the day's start with lassitude and dissension.

I am haunted by exquisitely precious images of you asleep, before cancer had invaded your body. So often you were on your side, with your fingers interlocked beneath your cheek. The pose, most of all, appeared prayerful. A knowing smile was forever caught in a precious stage of early blossoming. God seemed to be holding you in safe repose. In these moments, I especially thought of you as my angel on earth, in the hands of God.

At other times, you had your arms bent with your elbows extending outward, protecting your face at the gentle apex of the triangle. The back of your hands caressed your cheeks, your fingers curled softly under your chin. The pose was unusual and delicately evocative of a self-hug. Sometimes you would unbend your arms one at a time and, with the other hand, gently trace your fingers up and down the full length of your arm. You would gently stroke one arm and then the other. Usually, you returned your hands to your cheeks, recreating the protective triangle.

Before cancer, I would watch you in these peaceful poses for joyful hours of quiet and contentment.

These precancer sleep patterns seem so innocent and whimsical now.

Once you were delivered the cancer diagnosis, sleep for you quickly became a torturous form of high alert, a civilian form of military guard duty. Watchfulness usurped soothing withdrawal and restorative rest. Attenuating senses burned in place of repose.

For days and days on end, the unmitigated cancer diagnosis deleted sleep from your playbook. You needed time to process the news. You needed time to ponder why. You needed time to weigh the consequences; to pray; to accept the threat; to turn it into a challenge; to woman up your resolve; to sand down the sharp edges of the diagnosis; to learn to walk with a poisonous, rancorous enemy ransacking your cells and blood and sinews; to calm your urges to panic; to face your sons and hide your fear; to smile when every instinct called for tears; to stand tall when the prognosis called for sublimation.

You said no to sleep out of a sense that your wakefulness was a time to answer cancer's call with defiant prayer and deepening will to believe in a cancer-free future. Sleep would only interrupt your most graceful, mature response. Sleep would destroy your momentum of resolve and would necessitate rebuilding it, which would require even more energy—energy you no longer had. So you thought; so you felt. So you have my eternal admiration for how you have responded, for how you have courageously faced up to all the challenges cancer is giving you.

I remember my father talking about military guard duty, a seemingly insignificant topic in the context of the wars and carnage he endured though twenty-five years of military service. He talked of the brutal loneliness of it. He extolled the test it represented of doing the right thing when no one was around to witness or judge. He explicated the responsibility squarely on one's shoulders with no one around to complain to or blame. Boots laced tight, .45-caliber standard issue side arm cleaned, oiled, loaded, and at the ready. Uniform meticulously pressed and boots spit shined as a salute to the lasting influence of all the drills and training, and to satisfy one's own sense of pride and honor.

Post cancer diagnosis, your life has become a form of guard duty.

For both of us, everything about sleep is radically different. Some days, sleep never comes in any form. Your eyes will not close. Your body will not settle down. Your mind will not turn off. If sleep comes at all, it is only with an understanding that it will be short and fitful. It comes with an understanding that it will occur only as a last resort, only as the most grudging acquiescence. It is a small death that you long to delay for as long as possible, if not defeat outright.

I watch you fight sleep, knowing that its restorative and escapist properties have been maliciously corrupted along with your body's cells. I watch you fight it as simple acknowledgment that no physical position offers adequate relief from cancer's traveling, piercing, ravaging pain. I watch you sit up with your arms extended at absurd angles, bolstered by pillows, stymied from comfort. I watch you elevate your legs to just the right height, the right height as elusive as wind. I watch you in defeat, your head falling forward against your will, wishing I could aid your search for a restful, pain-free position in any small, humble way.

I listen to your breathing—heavy, labored, and uneven. I listen to your sighs, sometimes sharp, sometimes elongated, and always evocative of your will to fight. I watch you recline for a few moments, then sit up, and alternate these movements all through the night, to no avail of rest.

You are a warrior on guard. Sleep has ceased being a friend. Instead, it corners you against your will. It has become an unholy bargain, soulless, profane, wicked, and wretched.

Our bed has become another enemy that you must face. The mattress is unforgiving in its one-dimensional fact. Your body needs caressing envelopment that no inanimate object can satisfy. The sofa, with its contours and crevices, seems to offer more options for respite. Blankets and pillows now have more sophisticated structural roles. They no longer simply support and cover. Now, they must be enlisted in the effort to supply comforting pressure to the insistent points of blistering pain. Bedding must join with heating pads and ice packs and pain patches and massage to assuage the constant pain so that sleep has a chance actually to be sleep.

I think you are afraid that you will not wake from whatever fitful, restless surges sleep now provides. I imagine you fear waking with more pain and with less of a fighting chance against cancer's ever-imposing threat. I imagine you think sleep will leave you diminished rather than restored, and resuming the fight will be that much harder. I imagine that you cannot imagine that restoration of energy and resolve will ever come from what you now know as sleep.

I watch you as I have never watched you before. I hold you with my eyes. I hold you with my arms. I hold you with my heart. I hold you in my prayers.

I look for signs of healing. I measure your breathing with my own. I sigh in unison with your sighs.

I fearfully look for signs of diminishment, praying for signs of resurgence. I fight sleep alongside you.

For you, cancer has replaced sleep with fighting and searching and thrashing.

Like a soldier, you are being forced to fight cancer with little or no sleep.

Like a soldier, you are on endless guard duty.

Cancer writhes your body and, as your partner and witness, ravages my soul.

CHAPTER TWENTY-EIGHT

Conserving Strength

Heavy as a feather, light as an anvil, cancer has twisted and corrupted for you the dynamic of physical touch. An intended caress will cause you to flinch in near pain. In the realm of physical affection, you are a soldier showing signs of post-traumatic stress disorder. All your senses are attuned to defending against cancer's constant attack, and sometimes you can make no allowance for a soft, loving gesture, however innocent. Your guard stands ready for rebuff. The gates are up all the way; the mote seethes from floor to surface with hungry predators ready for encroachment. High alert round the clock. Nerves frayed. Permanently edgy. You're nearly always engaged in high-gear defense mode.

I understand, and I remind myself to avoid an unannounced touch. Even an announced touch is likely to be misconstrued. The feather morphs into an anvil. The touch is unwelcomed and crushing in its effect. You cannot bear the weight while you wage an all-out war against cancer. I understand. More importantly, you understand, and you do not hold my transgressions against me.

Sometimes touch of any kind unleashes emotions that you cannot afford to have unleashed. You simply do not have the strength to regather and refortify your emotions, much less to have so much strength expired in the actual unleashing. Like a soldier seeing his comrades fall, you don't have time or energy to expend your strength through an indulgent outpouring of emotion. You must keep moving to the next phase of war.

There are times when it is ill-advised for me to so much as ask you how you are doing. It is, after all, a rather stupid question, and one that must be annoyingly tiresome for you to answer in a way that hopefully deters additional stupid questions.

CHAPTER TWENTY-NINE

The Faustian Bargain

I wake in the middle of the night and look in your direction to see how you are handling the chemo. For a few seconds, I cannot see you in bed. I see the outline of the pillow, but not your head. I see the indentation, but no face or human outline. Just as I am starting to rise to look for you, I look again and then see you. What gives?

Was I asleep when I could not see you? Was I half asleep? Partly awake, partly dreaming? Hallucinating? It doesn't matter. What does matter is that chemo is laying you so low as to almost make you disappear. No optical illusions account for what I now observe in my fully awakened state. The bed seems to be swallowing you whole. Your body, as it absorbs the chemo, is being denigrated and diminished. The chemo kills cancer cells, but it also kills healthy cells in your blood, bones, organs, and flesh.

Chemo is the medical community's great Faustian bargain. It prolongs life, but at the same time, it diminishes life and ultimately extinguishes it. In the absence of a cure, the chemo treatment for you as a stage 4 patient is classified as palliative, meaning that it is designed to improve the quality of the patient's life and extend survival. Without chemo, death would be, barring a miracle, certain. With chemo, death remains certain, merely delayed.

In Martin Scorsese's 2006 film *The Departed*, one of the main characters, played by Jack Nicholson, in a small but poignant scene finds out that another character's mother is dying. The minor character says, "She's on her way out." Although the Nicholson character is a murderous mobster, he responds with eloquence, courage, and wisdom: "We all are, act accordingly."

You are "acting accordingly" in spades.

Through the first two years of your battle, you have not allowed chemo treatments to prevent you from working, from traveling to Indiana and New York, from walking several times per week, and from playing tennis, despite your oncologist's objections, who fears that you will fall and break increasingly fragile bones.

On the tennis court, you position yourself at the baseline with a defiant look. You are teasing but also challenging me to hit the ball past you. I am at best a middling, self-taught tennis player. I am used to public courts on a Saturday morning playing against equally mediocre friends. You are a collegiate scholarship player from Southwest Texas State University, a veteran of practice sessions and matches in triple digit temperatures and 90 percent humidity in San Marcos, Texas.

When I practice, I can achieve a moderately decent forehand that lands deep on a fairly low trajectory. For you, even diminished by chemo, you have little trouble returning my best shots. I am used to hitting to players' backhands, figuring that would be a weakness, as it usually is with hackers. But you are no hacker, with or without chemo soaking your system. In fact, your strength is the backhand shot, two-handed, a la Serena Williams. You have that lethal whipping action to your returns, which makes the ball jump with extra velocity and movement. Your forehand shots also whip over the net, all the way to the baseline. You know exactly where to stand; you anticipate where I'm going to hit the ball. Even with your limited movement, you are able to "pick" the ball off the court, no matter how close to your feet it lands. You pivot easily and seemingly catch the ball on your racquet just before you send it sizzling back to me. Off your whipping racquet, the ball zings across the net, and I imagine how formidable you were in college. I do not need to imagine how formidable you still are. I cannot do anything with your shots but be a backstop when

I don't miss them outright. At five feet nine inches, you can reach all my returns unless I get lucky and find a corner. Sometimes I hit to your backhand just to watch your perfect form and admire your proficiency.

Anything center court you return with smooth alacrity and ease. The only way I can win a point against you is by hitting to the corner. The chemo has not taken away your ground strokes when you can reach the ball, but it has taken away your lateral movement. If my shot is accurate, you simply watch it and give me a "thumbs up," and then you flip me the bird with your eyes. Chemo has taken way a step, but not your sense of humor. I suppress my competitive nature and try to hit in the middle of the court, where you can relive your athletic prowess that carried you away from what had become for you a claustrophobic Madison, Indiana, to the unlimited expanse of south central Texas. You defy cancer; you defy chemo. With or without hair, you hit stinging cross-court backhands that leave me feeling immobile and in awe of your ability to "act accordingly."

And then the tennis racquets sit in the garage, gathering cobwebs and spiders. Sometimes it is only you, the cancer, and the chemo fighting for supremacy. No room for me. I am on the sidelines, lost. You go because you must go. You fight because you love life. You count what you have left, and you refrain from feeling bitterness and anger over all that you have lost.

Pain stuns, drives you to a remoteness that I cannot bridge with attentiveness or empathy. The pain reigns supreme—arrogant in its domination, animalistic in its jealousy, proud in its ownership.

CHAPTER THIRTY

Tough Enough

In our last consultation with your first oncologist before he retired, he whispered to me on the way out of his office that as we fought cancer, we had to be tough. We were in your second year of treatment. Fortunately, you are plenty tough.

Chemo is analogous to getting into a head-butting contest with a bull. Forget riding the bull. That would be cake compared to cancer and its evil twin, chemo. You are tough enough to walk without drama up to the bull and commence head-butting. No fanfare, no audience, no applause, no sponsorships, no awards. Then, with dignity and pride intact, you crawl away with every cell in your body concussed, and somehow, you recover, only to do it all over again in a week's time.

Chemo is a handstand on knifepoints. Healing will most likely be a Pyrrhic victory.

You are tough enough to act, with cancer, like Prometheus. The difference is that you willingly chain yourself to the rock, welcoming the eagle to feed on your liver. You know all too well that with chemo, punishment equals preservation, though not eternally (mythology being infinite, medicine being finite), which does not in any way diminish your toughness.

You are Doctor Faustus with cancer, tough enough to meet Mephistopheles in the dead of night on a dead-end street to seal the bargain. Each and every time you open up your bloodstream to chemo, you are bargaining everything in search of a miracle.

You are tough enough to have had so many things taken away from you without losing your love of life: your breasts, your hair, your sense of taste, your appetite, your symmetry (edema has ballooned one leg to twice the size of the other), your balance, your mobility, your athleticism, your immune system, your vision, your ability to concentrate, your work, your ability to sleep peacefully, your pain-free existence. Yet you still fight on, care on, dream on, hope on, will on, inspire on, love on.

I suspect that your doctor doesn't need me to tell him that you are tough enough. I suspect that he was really talking to me.

CHAPTER THIRTY-ONE

A Perfect Human Prayer

I sit looking at one of your oncologist's reports. The first sentence quaintly describes you as a pleasant fifty-year-old woman. The quaintness ends quickly. The rest of the paragraph goes into clinical details about your progressive breast cancer, metastasized into lymph system, neck, bones, lungs, and liver. The paragraph also delineates the various chemotherapy treatments you have undergone and other drugs you have been prescribed, including estrogen blockers and bone strengtheners.

Irrationally, I am offended by that first sentence. It represents such an anemic attempt to humanize an otherwise objective robust report of your disease and treatment. I cannot resist a powerful need to amend the first sentence of the report. Beyond pleasant, you are

> my most compelling reason to breathe,
> my path to self-awareness,
> my second chance for a happy childhood,
> my answer to depressive, fatalistic instincts,
> my reason for senses awakened and attuned,
> my discovery that it is never too late,
> my connection between heart and head, my salvation on
> earth,
>
> an eternally inspiring flame, a perfect human prayer.

CHAPTER THIRTY-TWO

New York City

O ther than erring on the initial diagnosis of the lump in your breast proving to be a cancerous tumor rather than a benign cyst, you are remarkably prescient about the progression of your disease. Despite enduring surgery, radiation, and chemotherapy, your cancer in year 2 is showing no signs of slowing down. Your oncologist has made it clear that he will never be able to eradicate the cancer from your bones. The best he can do is slow its rapid growth, or better still, halt its progression completely. Essentially then, we are playing defense.

Therefore, when you said you wanted to take a trip while you were still able to travel, I resisted an instinct to dismiss your concern (denial is an enchanting siren) and instead tried to focus on where you were thinking of going. In this summer of the second year of your disease, you announced that you wanted to see New York City at Christmastime.

You foresaw an eventual day when walking for you would become an almost insurmountable ordeal. When moving from your hospital bed to the sofa, a distance of five feet, would require an hour to gather your will to make the move, an excruciating ten minutes to execute the move, and an hour to recover from the resulting stress and strain. But that day was not this day. This day you were still feeling strong and capable and ready to test yourself on a cross-country trip to one of the most exciting cities in the world, at what was your absolute favorite time of the year. You and I had been to NYC separately in our lives, but decades ago. Our sons had never been there. The thought of going together was enticing to all of us. Although you and I had minor trepidations about cold temperatures, our sons were full speed ahead in their outlook. For them, the hardest part of the trip would be waiting until Christmas. It was only August when you broached this wish.

My sister and her husband had traveled to NYC recently and recommended an upscale hotel perfectly located: the Park Lane Hotel, next door to the famed Plaza Hotel, on Central Park West. The Park Lane is property formerly owned and resided in by the famous Leona Helmsley, who surfaced in the news back in the '90s as a slumlord owner of assorted NYC apartment buildings. Despite the rather steep price for our budget, we decided to splurge, having been convinced by my sister that the location could not be surpassed. Central Park lies immediately to the north; Times Square, St. Patrick's Cathedral, and Fifth Avenue are all within easy walking distance.

As our two sons anticipated the trip to NYC, they otherwise spent the fall attending community college and high school. I worked through my twenty-seventh year of teaching. You held tightly to your positive outlook as you fought cancer honorably and gracefully and followed a treatment protocol of a capsule form of chemo, an estrogen blocker, and a bone-strengthening drug. You also geared up for our trip to NYC by taking mile-long brisk walks and keeping up with the usual assortment of domestic chores. No matter how much pain you endured, you insisted on maintaining a routine of laundry and housecleaning, including scrubbing floors on your hands and knees, cooking, and helping out with our high schooler's homework, especially math, Spanish, and anything requiring artwork.

Since we were going to be in NYC from the day after Christmas until New Year's Day, we put up our tree early in order to have more time at home to enjoy it. We put the tree up and accompanying decorations a week before Thanksgiving. Tacitly, as we decorated the tree, we both wondered how many more shared Christmases we would have. I'm proud of the way we both resisted the urge to become maudlin or melodramatic. At the same time, our private thoughts were a bit subdued and missing the normal unbridled exhilaration associated with unboxing ornaments and testing lights.

Humor emerges as more necessary and important when death hovers. In the taxi going from JFK International Airport to the Park Lane Hotel, you and the boys never stopped laughing at how terrified I looked sitting in the taxi's extra-vulnerable front seat. You all volunteered me for the front seat by jumping into the back before I knew what was happening. The usually exalted "shotgun" seat was given up no doubt for the first time ever by our two sons. During the hair-raising ride, you all put aside your own terror to enjoy mine.

The driver, of Indian descent, we learned, looked completely in his element of weaving, honking vehicles, intent on gaining ground at any cost, presumptively to prove driving prowess if not to shorten the journey. I felt as if we were trapped in a video game, rumbling and bumping over potholes and through inexplicably disappearing traffic lanes, construction zones, and graffiti-emblazoned concrete abutments. I have never relied so fearfully on a seat belt to hold me relatively upright. I doubt that you thought of cancer once on the hour-long thrill of a ride. Your sons kept you wedged in the middle of the rear seat, an especially good thing since you could not find a seat belt. I kept my left arm stretched between the two front bucket seats, and you held on to my arm as you would a rollercoaster roll bar.

Our first glimpse of NYC was thankfully after nightfall. The city glimmered unimaginably luminescent, with cavernous areas of darkness in the spaces between the skyscrapers. In the daylight these same skyscrapers would leave you feeling claustrophobic and depressed. But on this first night of arrival, we were enthralled by the glittering urban pearl laid out before us. We called out famous landmarks as we recognized them: the Chrysler Building, the Empire State Building, the newly built One World Trade Center, the Brooklyn Bridge. We felt like stereotypical tourists, but we didn't care. The cab driver ignored our sentiments. He was removed from us to his own world of navigation, contemplating, we would discover later, how exactly he would approach the Park Lane, knowing one-way streets would hamper an easy arrival. Our cabbie scared the life right out of us by taking a wrong turn down a one-way street. Amazingly, he stayed on it for what seemed like forever until he could turn off. His error in judgment left us, a few moments later, in front of our hotel but inconveniently across the cobblestone street. Our driver gave us an "oh well" shoulder shrug and popped open the trunk, our signal that we would have to pull our luggage across the street. We hardly cared. We were wholly consumed by the sights: horse-drawn open carriages; too many cabs to count yielding people on missions of business and leisure; doormen in full-length wool coats, white gloves, and top hats; and swarms of people entering and exiting Central Park.

No sooner had we checked in than our sons implored us to go out for a walk of exploration. They were understandably filled with excitement and thoughts of unpacking or resting after a twelve-hour trek, replete with a layover in Phoenix and a "Mr. Toad's Wild Taxi Ride," were just plain silly. I didn't care. I was open to doing anything that continued to make you feel like a person without cancer. On the flight from Bakersfield to Phoenix, you had said it felt so good to be leaving the environment where nearly all talk was about disease and treatment. In NYC the diverse and nonstop stimuli had already started serving as a grateful distraction from sickness. Besides that, you were as open to the idea of exploring the city as anyone. You did have one condition, which fit your personality. You insisted on unpacking your suitcase and storing your clothes in the lovely dresser. I joined you while the boys urged us to unpack faster.

Chemo had rendered you inert. This trip animated you. Freed you from the prison of cancer. Made you forget. On the concourse of the Phoenix airport during our two-hour layover, you walked up and down, deftly weaving in and out of travelers, checking out southwest trinkets, scoffing at overpriced food, and watching people. We eventually succumbed to the exorbitant food prices and bought the cheapest item we could find, offering meager sustenance for the five-hour flight to NYC: chicken snack wraps. We proudly staked claim to an area of carpet in the jammed waiting area and felt cozy leaning against our carry-ons. I felt grateful that you looked like anyone else in the airport. You were not a cancer patient in the battle of her life; you were simply a tourist with a plane ticket, waiting for her connecting flight. You too seemed lost in the moment, to have forgotten your plight. I prayed this was so.

After you and I unpacked in our room, while our boys waited impatiently, we all hit the streets, the boys leading. Within seconds, we were enmeshed in a mass of bodies in Rockefeller Plaza, staring in wonder at the stunning Christmas tree display, a sight we had all seen many times on TV but now were witnessing all the more impressively live. You attenuated your steps to follow your boys, enjoying their wonderment much more than your own. You had instigated the trip but had quickly given over your enjoyment to them, an act of vicarious unselfishness. Each time I looked at you, you were looking at them rather than at the sights we had come to see. I loved you for that graciousness more than I can tell you. This became the theme of the trip for you. Everything you experienced, you filtered first and foremost through our sons' experience.

Years later our reliving of the trip lives in your enjoyment of their enjoyment, despite the fact that we all went only because you wanted to go.

On New Year's Eve, we enjoyed a lovely early dinner at Patsy's, a well-known Italian restaurant in the Broadway District. We were enchanted by the photos of Frank Sinatra, Dean Martin, and countless other celebrities who had frequented Patsy's over the years. Our sons sat at the white-tableclothed table and acclimated to the high-class atmosphere with ease and aplomb. Again, your joy was secondary to their joy; your pleasure was wholly dependent on theirs, and thankfully, they were exactly where they wanted to be. After dinner, we roamed Times Square, flirting with sticking around until the ball dropped. After two hours of delightful roaming indecision, we opted to return to our hotel and escape the gathering hordes of revelers. Several people advised us that if we were going to partake of the famous celebration, we would benefit from adult diapers, as restrooms were out of the question with a million people huddled together. As tempting as that prospect loomed, we somehow resisted and settled for the comfort of the Park Lane.

Around 9:00 p.m., the boys were being called by the excitement out on the streets. You and I gave ourselves over to their whims, and we embarked on another adventure. The important point here is that you were adapting to their wishes without fear or hesitation. You were not a cancer patient. You were one of a million revelers on the streets looking for the perfect place to welcome in the New Year. With the aid of YELP, our boys discovered a wings bar on the Upper West Side. We walked in twenty-degree temperatures for at least twenty blocks before we found it. The trek proved well worth it. The bar was intimate and sparsely attended by what quickly became apparent were regulars. The owner had no problem with a minor in his establishment as long as we sat at a table and kept him away from the bar. We had found a perfect world. We had several TV monitors to share in the Times Square festivities; tasty, unpretentious snack foods perfect for our boys to balance Patsy's culinary sophistication; and an informal, welcoming atmosphere. At eleven thirty the owner passed out New Year's party favors and champagne flutes. At eleven forty-five, even our teenager had a glass of complimentary champagne. We sat and all felt cancer- free, most especially you. The waitresses could not have been kinder or more attentive. The customers were friendly and all smiles. The owner thanked us for coming in and told us to come back any time. We felt like New Yorkers, if only for an evening. Most importantly, you felt like a cancer-free New Yorker.

The thought of walking twenty blocks back to the Park Lane in seventeen-degree temperature was more than any of us wanted to endure. We had no trouble finding a taxi and were soon warmly ensconced in our beds, a stellar New Year dripping indelibly through our collective consciousness.

During our week in New York, you most enjoyed our boys going out on their own to explore the city. The oldest discovered all-night Asian markets and brought back to the room delicious sushi and delicate noodle dishes. Our youngest son loved the vibe on the street. We're sure they explored shops and sights that they have yet to share with us.

You discovered that NYC was not your cup of tea. The size and girth of the buildings disoriented you and gave you your first ever feeling of claustrophobia. The cold also shocked your system. The boys were unaffected by it; I was accepting of it and only mildly affected. Growing up in Pittsburg, I suppose, caused me to be less shocked by the extreme cold. I was also distracted from the cold by virtue of being in a completely different and fast-moving setting. For you, the wind whistling and whipping between the buildings was especially bothersome.

As much as you were disappointed by the effect of NYC on your senses and outlook, in my estimation, you triumphed over all the assorted obstacles we encountered during our trip. In the end, after the airline tags had been yanked from our luggage, that is what matters most to me and gives the greatest meaning to my memories of the experience.

Despite your disappointment in how the city made you feel uncomfortable and claustrophobic, you responded with enthusiasm to every adventure we embarked upon, and you were serenely elated at how much your sons loved New York. Cancer effaced as we raced like slapstick film actors to a reservation for a harbor boat tour. Somehow, we made it from the Park Lane to the southern tip of Manhattan with literally seconds to spare. A combination of subway, taxi, and running through vehicle and pedestrian traffic landed us at the right pier as only happens in the movies. The fact that it happened in our lives will forever stand as a victory over cancer for you in my mind, and hopefully, one day in your mind too.

Our taxi driver, once aware of our plight, broke numerous laws, including driving on highway shoulders, creating traffic lanes out of his daring imagination, eclipsing slow-on-the-draw drivers who apparently had time to burn, and performing hair-raising U-turns with James Bond élan. The driver's horn was in constant use, and he seemed to believe as much as we did that missing the harbor cruise was simply not an option. After all, this was a twilight cruise, the last of the evening, and waiting till tomorrow, though logical, lacked emotional fulfillment. The cancer in your blood, tissue, and bones was of no consequence as you jumped on and off the subway, ventured into dizzying traffic to help hail our taxi, and weaved in and out of pedestrian hordes to claim our place on the boat. We even managed to purchase a refrigerator magnet of the NYC skyline in the shape of the Big Apple as we approached the ticket window.

Our efforts were rewarded with a lovely experience, happily spent in the main cabin while our sons braved the exposed top deck until their lips turned blue and their fingers lost feeling and flexibility. The views of Manhattan Island from the water were immeasurably romantic and iconic: Wall Street, SoHo, Tribeca, Little Italy, the proud and defiant One World Trade Center. Cruising close to the Statue of Liberty with lights aglow seemed like something out of the movies. Motoring below the Brooklyn Bridge still seems like a fantasy. At the conclusion of the harbor tour, we took advantage of a free trolley bus ride to Times Square. You and our sons secured standing room in the lower enclosed section, heaters running thankfully, while I hesitated and got pushed to the exposed upper deck. I huddled in the front seat and tried to take advantage of the Plexiglas as a windbreak, to little effect. The hostess with the microphone, a diminutive senior citizen, and I survived the frigid temperatures by conversing during the gaps in her rehearsed presentation. Later, you all had a wonderful laugh at the sounds of my weather distress and inane commentary, picked up on her microphone and broadcast throughput the bus. The hostess could not have been more gracious.

You further triumphed in NYC by jockeying for position in Times Square, Rockefeller Center, and famous department stores, including FAO Schwarz and Bergdorf-Goodman. I dragged you and our sons selfishly through the Strawberry Fields section of Central Park when none of you had a real interest, other than indulging me. This indulgence extended to a walk around the famous Dakota apartment building while I relived the history of John Lennon's murder and mentioned the luminaries who called the Dakota home, such as the glorious actress Lauren Bacall. None of you cared, but you all got a kick out of how much I did. Again, I mark these experiences as your defiant stand against cancer and your will to live in the face of the disease's menace and degradation.

NYC, for all of us, will forever remain not merely a vacation but also a heroic statement by you that cancer is no match for human spirit, soul, will, and humble yet bold insistence on living.

Your reign of supremacy over cancer continued during a wild excursion by rental car from the heart of Manhattan to Allentown, a city in the mideastern area of Pennsylvania. The purpose of the trip was to meet one of your sisters-in-law, Chrissy, the wife of your brother Jeff. From the Park Lane, we subwayed and walked to the rental car shop on the Upper East Side of Manhattan.

A factor making the trip comical in a Laurel-and-Hardy kind of way was the fact that we towed a suitcase filled with dirty clothes, hoping to find a Laundromat somewhere along the way. The Park Lane is so upscale that the only laundry option is valet service, economically unpractical for the swarthy "range and mange" of one teenager and one twentysomething. You and I were used to lower-scale accommodations with coin-operated washers and dryers at our disposal. Embarrassingly, we earlier had rolled this suitcase through Lower Manhattan on the same mission, without success. Is anything more silly than advertising one's tourist identity with a bulky suitcase on recalcitrant wheels being dragged through the streets of Manhattan?

At any rate, we found the rental car shop with cell phone GPS, and you and the boys navigated to support my nervous driving. Truth told, I was still trying to overcome the emotional ramifications of driving in NYC in 1976 as a completely overwhelmed twenty-year-old, swallowed whole by the pace and aggressiveness of NYC traffic.

Thanks to expert iPhone navigation by the two millennials in our back seat, we rolled through the city and were viewing a blurry, misty Newark through steady rain. Soon, the verdant green of Pennsylvania welcomed our rental car, and Allentown was within sight.

After our reunion with your sister-in-law, we resumed our mission to find a laundry, unwilling to return to NYC with our luggage still filled with dirty clothes. Again, our sons guided us to a public laundry using their iPhones with only one U-turn necessary. As our clothes spun and tumbled, our eldest slept in the car, our youngest slept in the laundry, and you and I folded and stacked our mission to completion, all the while indulgently rejoicing in our undeterred spirit.

Back in the city, our rental car safely returned with a full tank of gas from a gas station somewhere on the Upper West Side, thanks again to our homegrown millennial navigators, we resumed our trek on the streets and subway, this time our suitcase somehow lighter with satisfyingly clean laundry.

As a final act of independent and wholly unsuspected joy, we discovered a vegan restaurant a few subway stops from where we returned the rental car. Our suitcase sat at the table with us as we delighted in an intimate establishment operated by highly efficient and conscientious twentysomethings.

We never could have scripted such a set of indelible experiences from NYC through New Jersey to Pennsylvania and then back to the Big Apple—our laundry clean, our memories rich and forever, cancer disinvited from our reality, your heart triumphant.

CHAPTER THIRTY-THREE

Photos

You taught me to see. You taught me to look for what is there and for what is not there. You showed me how to observe what is explicit in our physical world, as well as to recognize all those things that are implicit: shadows, reflections, projections. You especially taught me to see what I did not want to acknowledge due to immature fits of self-preservation, self-patronization, and denial.

Not long after we returned from our trip to NYC, you announced one day that you had scheduled us to meet with a local photographer to discuss having our pictures taken. I was flummoxed by your insistence that we needed to do this. Your decision, detached from an occasion such as an anniversary or birthday, seemed arbitrary. In theory, I was certainly not opposed to photos, but I was also caught off guard by your obvious haste.

The photographer could not have been more accommodating and charming. The pictures of other individuals, families, and landscapes in her modest studio and office were quite impressive, so much so that the worn-out, prosaic nature of the office itself had been transformed into an impromptu, vibrant "showing." You had obviously chosen an unassuming yet skillful and sensitive photo artist.

In our meeting, the photographer innocently inquired as to the impetus for the photos. You were ready for her question; I was blind. You stated simply, "As a stage 4 cancer patient, I want a record of who

I am physically before chemo takes its toll." The photographer began to tear up. Meanwhile, a lightning bolt of reality struck me.

Our moments together touching, side by side in front of the photographer, were the antithesis of what I had anticipated them to be. Rather than awkward and self-conscious, those moments were tender and enervating. My skin and body still reverberate years later with your weight against my side, with your smooth skin aligned with mine, with your body folding into my embrace.

Afterward, you explained more in a private seminar for me, your student. "I want the boys to remember their mom as she was before either the cancer or the chemo changes me beyond recognition. It's going to happen, you know. You're still in denial, and you need to face facts. I know you don't want to, but you're going to have to sooner or later. You can't fool yourself forever."

I cried in private later that night. I hid in the bathroom and tried to cut my tears with long swallows of beer. My wife, a woman wholly without vanity or ego, had been driven by cancer to have herself photographed for some future day when her sons, motherless, would have their sorrow fractionally eased by an image of the vibrant, full-of-life, beautiful mother they knew while growing up, hopefully supplanting the unmercifully altered image they would come to know as she lay dying.

CHAPTER THIRTY-FOUR

Ever the Wiser One

I don't know exactly when you internally accepted the reality that chemo was keeping you alive as it was also surely killing you. I do know that you grasped and swallowed that truth before I ever did. I was Ahab from the novel *Moby Dick* before awareness: when getting the whale reigned supreme, when triumph seemed possible. You were Ahab after awareness settled in: you would get the whale only by making the ultimate sacrifice.

On more than one occasion, you tried to persuade me that I had to accept facts: your struggle to overcome cancer was destined to fall short of my expectations. You always delivered your arguments gently and with a door open to miraculous intervention. You never sought refuge in fate. I now understand all too well that you were primarily urging me to prepare myself for the inevitable. Even in your darkest moments, when your life lay exposed in your consciousness fully in all its tragic vulnerability, you endeavored to protect me, to think of my well-being, to subvert your needs to mine.

I can only promise you that for the rest of my life, I will try to become worthy of such consideration.

CHAPTER THIRTY-FIVE

Edema

Cancer patients know all too well how the disease acts as a catalyst to other health problems. One common issue cancer patients often confront is edema, the retention of fluids in certain areas of the body. When a breast cancer patient has lymph nodes removed along with the breast, edema typically results in the arm on the side of the body where the nodes and breast were taken.

In your case, edema never occurred in your arm; instead, it developed in your right leg. As cancer spread throughout your body, tumors developed in the lymph system in your pelvic area, most suspiciously in the right groin. This made it difficult for water and blood to flow up from and out of your right leg.

The swelling first became noticeable in your ankle. We had been sitting together on the sofa, watching television. You held up your legs side by side, and one ankle was obviously much larger than the other. You had experienced swollen ankles before, resulting from a sprain or while pregnant. But those occasions were nothing comparable to this. Your ankle was so swollen that it appeared to have a tumor falling over the top of your foot and also over the outer side, close to the bottom of your heel.

The swelling that began in your ankle gradually extended up your leg, first enveloping your calf and then your thigh. The swelling then consumed your entire foot, including your toes.

For two years, edema plagued you. Eventually, it extended to your hips, first your right and then your left. It sometimes involved your left leg as well. But it mainly and consistently affected the right side of your lower body.

We went through the usual procedure of having you raise your legs above your head when you would sleep. You also received a wrapping treatment in which a doctor wrapped your entire leg from foot to groin in gauze. This wrapping was intended to put steady pressure on your leg to squeeze fluid up and out. We also massaged your leg several times each day. Additionally, your oncologist prescribed Lasix, the brand name of the drug furosemide, meant to rid your body of excessive fluid.

Except for the Lasix, nothing worked very well. The edema never disappeared. Sometimes, we thought the massage treatment worked, but never to a desirable degree. The problem with Lasix is that the drug is hard on one's kidneys. Your oncologist explained that he had to walk a fine line between helping you lose the excess fluid and damaging your kidneys. As with so many treatments and medicines, the side effects pose nagging and sometimes debilitating health issues and risks.

At its worst, the edema caused your right leg to grow to twice the size of your left. The contrast was exacerbated by the fact that your chemo treatments were causing you to lose muscle mass and bone density. You reached a point where your left leg was emaciated and your right leg was horrifically swollen to the degree that you could barely lift it off the ground. For a solid year, you could not wear a shoe. In winter, we bought a type of men's Ugg in a size 13, comically larger than your normal size 10 in a woman's fit. At least you could get the boot over your swollen foot.

Aside from your odd appearance, with one leg dwarfing the other in size, walking became extremely difficult for you. Your body lost its symmetry, causing you to stumble on occasion, fall, and generally have trouble with your balance. When you were in your weakest condition, the weight of your oversize leg became too much for you to lift into bed. I had to help you. Even when you were in bed, I had to help you move your leg as you needed to adjust your position.

Eventually, you could not lift your swollen leg high enough to navigate a curb. Even with my help, your preferred a handicapped walkway to a curb. Your swollen leg caused you to suffer more than one face plant. On one occasion, we were walking into an auto parts store. One moment, we were side by side talking and walking. The next instant, you were sprawled out on the pavement, cursing your edema and fighting back tears. Somehow you kept your face from hitting the pavement, but your palms, elbows, and knees bore the cost. You handled such moments with more grace than I could imagine or display. We got you back to the car, and I proceeded to the store alone. By the time I rejoined you, you were laughing about the incident.

Cancer adeptly and cruelly takes away both big and small things. Not satisfied having taken away your easy mobility and equilibrium, it also took away your enjoyment of shoes. I used to tease you when I would see a shoe catalogue with pages dog-eared. Despite an already impressive array of all types of shoes, dress, sport, sandals, and Vans, you could not resist adding another choice to your collection. Cancer limited you to walking without shoes when weather permitted, flip-flops when your swelling subsided, or a pair of ungainly Uggs, three sizes too big, transforming your natural stride into a kind of snow-shoeing effect in which your feet barely left the ground.

CHAPTER THIRTY-SIX

Your Undying Love Affair with Life

I will never know the source of your unrestrained and deeply abiding love of life. It was one of the things about you that initially caught my attention and attracted me to you. The cliché "She had a love affair with life" fits you more perfectly than any other statement I can think of. You viewed life as a gift, another cliché, but nonetheless true. You viewed life with a child's uncorrupted and unbridled sense of wonder and delight.

Although mornings were not your favorite time of the day, you always awakened with a smile and a sense of playful mischief. You had a unique talent to transform everything into a box of toys. The bed and all its accouterments immediately became playthings in your childlike, splendorous reverie. You built forts, you played hide-and-seek under the covers, you exiled me in response to imagined offenses, and you called me home whimsically. You loved waking up and then pretending you were still asleep. You demanded that I rate your "performances" as Oscar-worthy, Oscar-nomination-worthy, or Oscar-snub worthy.

You loved teasing each moment for wisps of laughter and enjoyment. No matter how heavy the world, you sought lightness through innocence, humor, and optimism. You resurrected statements made by your boys over the years that, as non sequiturs, rendered moments of stress, disappointment, and turmoil absurd and unimportant. Bits of a four-year-old's dialogue, such as "I have cash" or "This gum is spicy," never failed to elicit laughter and joy when they were needed most. You only allowed yourself to wallow in what was truly important and life-affirming and life-sustaining. You were wholly intolerant of negativity, self-indulgence, and self-pity.

You loved people. No, you did not view the world through rose- colored glasses, but you never lost your faith in the power of forgiveness and in redemption. You knew evil firsthand, but you never overlooked or lost faith in goodness and decency.

You loved sitting next to my father on the sofa and listening to his stories over and over again. You did not care that you had heard them so many times that you could tell them as well as he could, maybe better. Later, you sometimes told me of the parts he had left out. You delighted in his act of remembering and reliving. You loved walking with my mother as she struggled with her balance and recited her physical ailments. You calmed her with a steady, gentle hand and loving heart. You were at your best when extending simple courtesies to people in quiet moments when no one else listened or cared. You focused when others were distracted. You delighted when others were too self-absorbed to lend an ear. You sat when others scurried. For you, a simple conversation served as the kind of vicarious experience most others only knew through movies or amusement park thrill rides.

In Alice Walker's novel *The Color Purple*, a conversation between Celie and Shug symbolizes your love of and reverence for God and his world. Shug says to Celie, "I think it pisses God off if you walk by the color purple in a field somewhere and don't notice it." You always noticed and always appreciated God's fields of purple. You never ever pissed God off by failing to love and revere the world and all of its magical, mystical wonders, small and large. In brief, isolated moments, cancer surely tested your resolve to love life and appreciate the world, but its occupation and manipulation of your sensitivities ultimately failed to diminish your unyielding, undying love for and appreciation of life. Cancer could not diminish or mortalize your love affair with life.

CHAPTER THIRTY-SEVEN

Pain

For several years, we were able to keep your breast cancer from spreading beyond your bones. That limitation of your cancer's seemingly inevitable advance stood as a moral as well as physiological victory in your mind as the patient and for me as your caregiver. From the onset of your treatment, your care had been classified as palliative, meaning that you were a terminal patient. We received that classification as official, as something your doctors were duty-bound to say; however, we rejected it on the basis of our faith in God, on the basis of our faith in your resiliency, and on the basis of the power of your positive attitude.

Your oncologist described your fight against cancer as a war of attrition. We were playing defense. The cancer would surely advance; we would try to slow its advance to a crawl, guarding against an out-of-control onslaught.

The thought of playing only defense did not sit well with us, to say the least. We both felt that we were engaged in a fight that required not only a medical response but a spiritual and mental response as well. We trusted your doctors and nurses to provide the medical treatment, but we relied on each other to augment the medical treatment with prayer, faith, a sense of humility and humor, and mental tenacity. You and I also read and studied your disease so we were prepared to ask pertinent questions, understand and evaluate your doctors' decisions, and make intelligent suggestions when appropriate. In this process, we would be as informed and active as possible.

Your first oncologist let us know during your second year of treatment that your cancer was refusing to relinquish its aggressiveness, despite chemo, surgery, and radiation. It moved into your bones by the end of year 2, specifically your pelvis and your spine. We quickly learned that the chemo treatments were causing and accelerating the spread of arthritis as an unavoidable side effect. We also learned that chemo treatments lessened the pain caused by the cancer in your bones and the arthritis. During periods when you were not undergoing chemo, the pain became intolerable. During chemo, the pain was more manageable.

To help you withstand the pain, which your oncologist had warned us would become absolutely debilitating and excruciating, you were prescribed hydrocodone-acetaminophen and Fentanyl pain patches. You were then escalated to Valium as a painkiller. On your own, you would take Extra Strength Tylenol. The Valium proved ineffective. It also affected you mentally in a most pernicious way. You experienced hallucinations; you had trouble transitioning from dreams to consciousness. You became "whacky" (your own lexicon), finding it difficult to concentrate or follow the thread of a normal conversation. Following the plot of a movie or even TV show also became difficult.

The pain patches were effective, but you were supposed to change them only every seventy-two hours. Sometimes the patches would come off of their own accord before the seventy-two hours were up. Moisture from showers or sweating would often loosen them. Sometimes you needed patches in more than one area at a time, but you were only supposed to use one at a time. For two years you struggled to make the combination of hydrocodone, Valium, and patches work. Midway through your fourth year of treatment, you were prescribed morphine as your pain had become insufferable. You never stopped taking Tylenol on your own. Sometimes it seemed the Tylenol was more effective than anything else. Talking, hoping, and praying helped you endure the intense agony when pharmaceuticals failed.

Your ability to withstand pain was simply extraordinary. The adjustments you made to lessen the intensity of the pain were inhuman. Lying flat either on your stomach or your back became nearly impossible. For about a year, you were able to lie on your side in a fetal position with a pillow between your knees, but you would have to change sides each hour. You preferred the sofa to our bed. You generally hated being alone and never wanted to be in a room by yourself. We made a silly game of turning you from one side to the other. I would fluff your pillows with exaggerated movements and shenanigans, reminiscent of Ed Norton in *The Honeymooners*. You would indulge in my attention and mostly useless machinations, playing the role of the pampered queen. In reality, you were masking excruciating pain and the depressingly limited choice in tolerable sleep positions. I spent extra time massaging your head and shoulders and nuzzled your neck and gently kissed your cheeks and forehead.

The day arrived when you could no longer sleep in a prone position. Our oversize L-shaped couch allowed you to sleep sitting upright with your legs fully extended, easing the pain in your back and pelvis. You endured this accommodation to pain for several weeks, thankful that chemo reduced the pain and grateful not to be isolated in a bedroom with pain and discomfort as your only companions. I slept on the floor right below you. You would often wake me during the night when pain or restlessness prevented you from sleeping or when your overall situation became overwhelming. But some nights you suffered without waking me. I will never know how many nights you chose to let me sleep. I fear the number is more than I would like it to be.

I raised the option of purchasing a home hospital bed. You resisted. Such a step represented a development in the progression of your cancer that you understandably did not want to accept. You said you were comfortable with me researching and pricing beds, but you wanted me to hold off making a purchase.

CHAPTER THIRTY-EIGHT

Lightness: What Army Am I In?

I hold your head, and I am frightened to my core. Every time I hug you or cradle your head, you feel lighter. I argue with myself that this lightness does not mean what in my naked heart I know it means. Your head feels almost soft; it is as if I can feel your brain. I know I can't really, but my hands believe they can. Are. Instinctively, I want to hold on to you tighter, envelop you, protect you. At the same time, fear compels me to withdraw—an urge I rebuff only with all my mental fortitude. With fear tearing at my will, your lightness is too heavy to hold. But I force myself.

I can nearly hug you and myself at the same time; that is how emaciated your upper body is becoming. I detest the feel of my own hands circling back to my own arms. As we embrace, I can feel your comprehension in the way your face pushes into my neck. Sometimes tears roll down my chest, and I am deafened by their silent screams. Selfishly, I die inside.

> what army am I in?
> the briefings snarl endlessly
> dropping bromides of false hope,
> so easy to be seduced, entrapped;
>
> what office do I salute?
> if I must clear your way to higher hope,

to the flat-out edge of earthly pain,
where you can wink your cancer away.

what remembered formation
do I synchronize with?
alone now, left behind,
in steps that hear no cadence.

CHAPTER THIRTY-NINE

Spirit and Soul Forever Cancer-Free

I don't know when you realized that nothing your doctors could do would ever neutralize cancer long enough for you to regain some sense of physical capability. We knew in year 5 of your treatment that cancer would forever be a fact of your physical existence. But we held tight to the hope that the disease could be denied further advancement at the expense of your ability to function with a modicum of normalcy.

For me to pinpoint exactly when you realized that your doctors were overmatched by cancer's irrevocably malicious intent and underequipped with available drugs and treatments remains irrelevant. What is essential for me to explain is the shift in your sense of how you would handle this unimaginably grim reality. Only in retrospect do I understand how you redefined your true mission in battling cancer. While you never willingly surrendered your body to the disease and you continued to fight day to day and cell to cell, you established more important priorities. Namely, you would never allow the despicable disease to invade and compromise your beautiful spirit, your unyieldingly positive attitude, your love of people, your love of life, your belief in forgiveness and healing, and the inviolability of your soul.

While your doctors proved unable to draw a physiological line that cancer could not cross, you effectively and emphatically drew the spiritual line that you would never allow cancer to cross. You defended that line with a soldier's fealty to mission.

Before cancer, you were the most loving, positive, appreciative, empathic person I had ever known. After cancer, you remained the most loving, positive, appreciative, empathic person I had ever known.

* * *

Darlene taught elementary and middle school for ten years in the Mojave School District. But the most important lesson she taught the world was how to live with love and compassion for all and how to endure a physically debilitating disease with grace, dignity, and wisdom. She also demonstrated how to prevent that disease from becoming spiritually, emotionally, and mentally debilitating.

Born on April 7, 1965, in Madison, Indiana, Darlene learned from her parents, brothers, friends, and teachers the Midwestern values of humility, hard work, loyalty, and integrity, and she humbly displayed and spread those values to everyone she encountered throughout her fifty years of blessed life.

Darlene first and foremost dedicated herself to her sons, John-Michael and Trent. She loved them unconditionally and worked every day to prepare them for life's most intense challenges and tribulations. As Darlene fought cancer with a ferocious spirit and undaunted will, she was inspired by her sons' emotional maturation and intellectual development and always sought one more hug, one more conversation, one more opportunity to say "I love you." She wisely counseled them about how to reconcile her death and live honorably with a mother who would forever remain in their hearts.

Darlene did not have friends so much as she had spiritual sisters and brothers. She considered it her privilege to know and love her spiritual sisters and brothers with undying respect and devotion.

The earthly cause that Darlene remained committed to until her final breath was the well-being of her family. She thought about and prayed for her parents and three biological brothers—Mike, Jeff, and Cary—every day that I knew her. Geographical distance from her family pained her, but Darlene kept all her family members emotionally close in her mind and heart with religious conviction.

Darlene loved life as a precious gift from God. She loved profoundly and deeply all the people in her life, including her students from her decade of teaching. She kept them in her heart with admiration, respect, and wholehearted commitment to their happiness, safety, and well-being.

No one can properly explain how much physical, emotional, mental, and spiritual strength Darlene showed as she battled cancer. She never felt sorry for herself; she never became bitter. She never played the victim. She never lost her sense of humor; she never let go of her sense of optimism. Darlene never allowed cancer to compromise or diminish her love of life.

Cancer is weaker for having chosen Darlene as an opponent.

Darlene taught so many important lessons for people to contemplate and try to live up to: live without ego, love people with open arms and an open heart, make the world a better place for our children, regard every moment of life as a sacred blessing from God, remain forever positive, forgive enemies with compassion, stay strong when weakness beckons, and trust and embrace God's plan even when we don't fully understand it.

CHAPTER FORTY

Bell's Palsy

Toward the end of your fifth year of standing toe to toe with cancer and trading punches, you developed a condition that I knew nothing about and had barely heard of: Bell's palsy. I came home from work one day to find you sitting on the couch and showing in your face what appeared to be signs of a stroke. The left side of your face had abruptly collapsed. Your bottom lip suddenly looked uneven. You could not completely close your mouth. Your chin was awkwardly and newly creased. Your left eye would not blink or close. To say that your eyes betrayed perplexity would be a severe understatement.

As I absorbed the physical changes in your countenance since I had said goodbye to you that morning, you calmly asked, "Do you think I've had a stroke?" I sat down next to you and hugged you without saying anything. I asked you if you had any tingling or paralysis in your arms or legs. You did not. I asked you if you were able to recall the events of your day. You were. I asked if you thought you were slurring your speech. You did not think so. Listening to your pronunciation at that moment indicated that while your words sounded different due to your drooping lip, you were not slurring your speech in a way that suggested a stroke.

Resting on the sofa next to you was the *Mayo Clinic Family Health Book, Third Edition*. This weighty volume had been your constant companion for as long as I had known you, never more the object of your close studying than since your cancer diagnosis. You had read and reread the section describing the symptoms of Bell's palsy during the day and had already self-diagnosed your condition. Our conversation served only to confirm what you had already concluded: no stroke, but the annoying and troubling onset of Bell's palsy.

Together we reread the section in the Mayo Clinic tomb and agreed that you had correctly diagnosed your condition. One telling sign was that the paralysis on the left side of your face extended up to your forehead. This is not typically a consequence of paralysis caused by a stroke. The effect was to eliminate any wrinkles on your left side of your forehead. Your skin there was smooth and taut. The right side of your forehead looked normal, meaning wrinkles were evident.

As a precautionary measure, we scheduled an appointment with your oncologist that week and also scheduled an appointment with your eye doctor. We learned from our reading that you would need to take special care of your eye for the duration of your Bell's palsy. This would entail bandaging the eye and using eye drops to prevent the eye from drying out and becoming infected. Losing the ability to blink meant that your eye would not produce tears, so ointments would be necessary.

When your oncologist and optometrist each saw you, both reacted in exactly the same way: "You have Bell's palsy." They both let slip out a kind of wry laugh, as if to say, "What more can you endure?" This was a question that passed lightly from the lips of healthy men. For you, the question had settled in your psyche as an existential threat. It had become yet another front in your war against cancer. For your doctors, the question was professional, theoretical. For you, the question was all too personal, its answer inching closer day by day.

To prevent infection in your eye, we used eye patches every night and during the day when your eye became dry and scratchy, resulting from the cessation of tear production. A healing ointment kept your eye moistened, reducing the risk of ulceration.

The medical book informed us that Bell's palsy could last from weeks to months, up to a year. The possibility that it would never go away also existed, though permanency was rare. However, you were obviously not strictly a Bell's palsy patient. Your immune system had been seriously compromised by cancer and chemo. We lived knowing that in your case, the palsy might very well be permanent.

Through this ordeal, we tried to keep a sense of humor. With your eye patch in place, pirate jokes were unavoidable, though they quickly became stale. You joked that you would not need a Halloween mask as long as the Bell's palsy remained.

In more serious moments, you noted without self-pity that you now had a "mangled face" to go along with a bald head and a deteriorating body. Your use of the word *mangled* was a departure from your typically stoic attitude toward your situation. The word caused me to hemorrhage emotionally. For you, the word reflected a sense of being overwhelmed by the ancillary effects of your cancer—out-of-control edema in the legs, hips, and feet; compromised immune system; loss of taste and appetite; loss of hair, including eyebrows; dry heaves and vomiting; constipation; frequent urination due to the drug Lasix; skin rashes; weakening arm and leg strength; unrelenting pain; inability to sleep; and increasing inability to concentrate. Taken separately, these effects were relatively manageable. But collectively, they were insufferable.

You were learning to function with one eye. Reading and even watching TV had become more labor intensive. You were struggling with depth-perception difficulties. Driving had become more problematic than you could safely deal with, except in an emergency.

Without your patch, you developed a habit of closing your eye with your fingers. Sometimes you would hold your eye closed until it produced tears, giving relief from the dryness and scratchiness. As the months wore on, you would ask me to watch as you tried to blink. You struggled monumentally to move your eyelids. You lower lid held fast. Your upper lid would flutter a bit but remain lifted. Your eye would move involuntarily to the left, the pupil nearly disappearing. My heart broke each time you asked me to watch these attempts.

You learned from your parents that your Uncle Johnny, your mother's brother, had Bell's palsy twice. Each time, it went away in a few months, thankfully leaving virtually no trace that it had ever chosen him as a victim. This news gave you hope that you too would one day be free of this random, inexplicable condition.

We lamented but tried to laugh about the reality that one by one, you were being robbed of your five senses, which under ordinary circumstances, we take for granted.

You were becoming increasingly self-conscious about your overall appearance and lack of physical balance and coordination. Your world was shrinking at an alarming pace. Texting became an activity that consumed more and more of your time. From your hospital bed in our living room, you held your phone constantly and texted family and friends incessantly. This evolved as your way to stay connected and informed. The prospect of venturing outside was rapidly losing viability and enticement.

I would never describe you as a vain person. Bell's palsy had not "mangled" your face, as you so often remarked, but it had made basic functions, such as seeing, blinking, drinking, eating, and swallowing absurdly awkward and difficult. Doing any if these things in the company of friends and strangers had become even more awkward and difficult. Though not vain, you were understandably self-conscious. The last thing you wanted to do was appear to be struggling in public, thus evoking pity. You possessed absolutely no tolerance for such an occurrence.

Watching you pinch your lips together on the side of your face that had become paralyzed so that you could sip liquid through a straw on the unaffected side, to me, was tragically heartbreaking. I could barely watch you going through this routine every time you wanted to drink.

Psychologically, Bell's palsy is testing you beyond reason. I think, without letting you know, that you have a right to ask God why so many challenges at once are bombarding you. But you never have such thoughts, and you never give in to such immature impulses, as I am inclined to do in moments of weakness. You go about your journey that seems to be about discovering exactly how many maladies and how much pain you can endure. Unemotionally, you tell me to stock up on straws. The Bell's palsy may last a year, or it may be permanent given your compromised immune system. You are moving through today's pain with unwavering grace and resiliency. You are preparing for tomorrow's challenges with one-eyed optimism.

CHAPTER FORTY-ONE

Daily Triumphs

All your life you have been self-sufficient, resolute, and resourceful. Cancer disrespects these qualities and targets them with pernicious rage and relentless aggressiveness. You respond by swallowing hard, reaching within your historically deep reservoir of independence and resiliency, and setting out to accomplish each day as much as your body will accommodate. Without vanity or ego, and with a marvelous sense of humor, especially given the circumstances, you meet me at the door daily to show me what you have been able to do while I have been at work. You engage in this ritual with a young girl's sense of bright-eyed optimism and a dying woman's sense of destiny. You hold no grudges, and you delight in daily chores and activities that most people would consider mundane and unworthy of mention or attention but what to you have become triumphal duties.

Laundry folded meticulously and piled high and neatly on our bed is your badge of honor and victory on many days. You walk me to the bedroom with glee sparkling in your eyes, equally in the one that still blinks naturally and the one that doesn't. I must remind myself to slow my pace to mirror yours. You like to hesitate just before we enter the bedroom to view your work. You ask me what I expect to find. I pronounce, with unbridled pride in your determination and stamina, "More clean laundry than is humanly possible for anyone to produce in a single day." You beam with what I can only describe as God's grace. I hug you and never want to let you go.

On other days, you ask me what I notice as soon as I enter our house. I pretend that I have not noticed that the carpets are freshly vacuumed, the tiled floor freshly dust-mopped. I make a game of it with you, feigning ignorance. I watch you watch me surveying the rooms. I want to delay giving you the answer that you cannot wait for me to give you. I want to extend the time when you can enjoy the anticipation of showing me what you have managed to accomplish while enduring unimaginable pain and mental anguish. When I finally acknowledge your achievements, you absolutely smile and gush your cancer away for a few delicious seconds. My heart breaks to see you so proud of things so small and now so large. I pray that you will break my heart again on more tomorrows than I can anticipate or count.

CHAPTER FORTY-TWO

Parents: Looking for You, Not Me

Y our parents, Mike and Phyllis Everidge, have driven from Indiana to California, a trip of over 2,100 miles, several times over the years to visit us. They are rugged, disciplined travelers, always making the trip in four crisp days. They set their mileage goals for each day, stop in the same places depending on weather and road construction, and usually stay in the same motels. Their planned and preferred itinerary goes as follows: the first leg runs from Madison, Indiana, to Joplin, Missouri; the second leg goes to Santa Clara, New Mexico; the third leg runs to Kingman, Arizona; and the last leg gets them to Tehachapi, California. They are on the road by daylight, and they avoid driving at night. As septuagenarians, their stamina to keep on the road and faithfully execute their precise driving schedule astounds us.

We are also astounded by the typically short duration of their visits. They love and miss their hometown of Madison in Southern Indiana along the Ohio River, and after about a week, they are anxious to return home. We beg them to stay, arguing that all the driving warrants a longer visit. We typically lose the argument. Home calls them like a siren's tempting song.

When they are with us, we spend hours upon hours sitting and talking. They are "old school" conversationalists. We talk about everything under the sun—books, politics, the world, culture, history, the weather, your hometown goings-on, states of personal health, and your brothers and their families. Your parents are attentive and patient listeners. They concentrate fully on the person speaking. They are free of facial expressions or mannerisms that indicate impatience to interject their own comments. When it is their turn to speak, they start slowly and thoughtfully. They are reflective and responsive to the details of the conversation. They ponder quietly. They actively "mine" conversations for bits of wisdom and revelations. I thoroughly enjoy listening to you and your parents reminisce about experiences from your childhood and events in your hometown. The memories that you share are rarely contradictory.

Your parents informally but effectively have taught their grandsons so much history and culture and so many life lessons through their personal stories of growing up and living in earlier decades. Your parents delight in sharing their deep reservoir of love for John-Michael and Trent and like nothing better than hearing about their latest thoughts and experiences.

Your father spent two nights during one visit helping Trent form with clay a representation of early-American family life. I recall an impressive product consisting of several realistic forms of family members, tools, and furniture. The outcome of the elementary school project displayed amazing detail and complexity. Your father shaped the clay with meticulous fidelity to the assignment's expectations, to details he thought were essential, and he happily poured into the project limitless love for his grandson. Your mother stayed close to the project, offering warm words of encouragement and helpful suggestions.

On many visits, we spend our evenings playing board games. We sit on the floor, munch on snacks, laugh with abandon, and tease one another with playful joy. Our favorite games are Trivial Pursuit, Apples to Apples, Sorry, Pass the Pigs, and Would You Rather? This last game produces moments of embarrassment that melt away the age differences among us.

Your father loves acting in an irascible, curmudgeonly manner to annoy you and your mother. On an unforgettable trip to Cambria, we all play 20 Questions in the car. On one of your father's turns, he selects "vegetable" as his category. You, Trent, your mother, and I are completely stumped after our twenty questions. Your father's specific item turns out to be a map, as in a state or regional road map. In response to our objections, he tries to rationalize the appropriateness of his selection of a map as consisting of paper, thus having its origins as a vegetable (tree). Your mother, Trent, and I are unconvinced, but you are fuming. You declare that never again will you play 20 Questions with your father. You judge him to be irrational, insane, impossibly stubborn, and deserving of scorn and ridicule. Your father could not be more satisfied that he has driven you to the height of frustration and annoyance.

In Cambria, at a simple yet lovely motel on Moonstone Beach Drive, with the beautiful Pacific as our front porch, your father again drives you to your wit's end. In the motel lobby, a table is set up with complimentary snacks and beverages, replete with fresh fruit, delicious muffins, cheese, water, juice, and coffee. In embarrassment, you watch your father make several trips across the parking lot to refill his plate and cup. In reality, he only made three return visits to the lobby, but to your senses, it seemed like six or seven trips. "Doesn't he know that there are other guests here who also would like something? He is cleaning them out. What's wrong with him? I cannot step foot in the lobby again. Go talk to him and tell him to leave something for someone else." I try to ease your ire and embarrassment by taking a long walk on the beach with you and Trent. I have always wondered if your father made all those trips across the parking lot, knowing that you were watching him, or if he was truly famished.

In the following days, you enjoy watching your parents play with Trent at the beach and laugh at his antics in the surf. We all take long walks on the beach, through the lovely town, and enjoy wonderful meals. You never do return to the lobby.

During your parents' final trip to California, before cancer had ravaged your appearance and physically debilitated you, your father became deathly ill. His sickness began with a stomachache, turned into nonstop vomiting, and eventually required surgery for an intestinal blockage and an extended hospital stay, including several days in the ICU. Ironically, the purpose of the trip was for your parents to offer you care and solace. We all became caretakers for your father. You risked your own health willingly and lovingly to support your mother and help care for your father. I believe it benefitted you to have a mission beyond fighting cancer.

Your mother stayed with your father for nearly the entire time he was in the hospital. She slept sitting up in an absurdly uncomfortable chair for over two weeks. She took sponge baths in the hospital's public restroom. Your mother's love for your father is core-of-the-earth deep. The only place she could be was by your father's side. Once your father was out of danger, we begged her to leave the hospital and get a good night's sleep in a bed. She refused.

When your father was still in the ICU, your brother Cary flew out from Houston to lend a hand. He was able to convince your mother to leave the hospital to get some much-needed rest in a real bed. Since our home was an hour's drive from the hospital, Cary got hotel rooms for your mother as well as for you so that she would not feel so far away from your father. Cary and your mom shared a room, and you stayed in another room. When Cary finally left after your father was out of the ICU, you and your mother shared a room for a few days. I will never be able to thank Cary sufficiently for flying out to help take care of your parents and for easing the burden you felt in trying to trying to assuage your mother's legitimate fears about your father's health and also to help your mother take care of her own physical health. You and I could not convince her to leave the hospital. Cary saved the day and only confirmed the limitless love and admiration you have always had for him.

After his release from the hospital, your father convalesced at our home with the aid of a physical therapist that thankfully made house calls. Your father needed to restore muscle tone, strength, and flexibility. He also needed to practice getting up and out of a chair, as well as into and out of a car. We all encouraged him to follow through on his prescribed regimen of weights and exercises. You and I delighted in the way your father would noticeably slack off when your mother was out of the room and then rediscover exuberance for his workout routine when your mother was in the room. Your father's love for your mother is core-of-the-earth deep, and he would not have ever wanted her to know that he was cheating a bit on his physical therapy. We kept that secret to ourselves.

Prematurely from our perspective, your parents returned to Indiana. Once again, they heard the siren's call.

In the late stages of your illness, you spent countless hours on the phone talking to your parents. You especially spent long hours on the phone with your mother. I knew with too much certainty that you were saying goodbye. Your father's health prohibited them making another trip to California. He was dealing with intensive follow-up care to his surgery, as well as blood pressure fluctuations, dizziness, and vertigo.

If you had asked your parents to return to California, I know with surety that they would have. The unvarnished truth is that whenever your parents would offer to make another trip out, you discouraged them vehemently. You wanted to spare them from seeing the deterioration you were sustaining. You wanted them to remember their daughter as you were in all your beautiful vibrancy.

CHAPTER FORTY-THREE

Indignities

While your strength lasts, you develop an interest in cooking. With your unbreakable desire to stay useful, you create delicious chili, various chicken dishes, one rich with curry and vegetables, and assorted desserts, including blueberry and chocolate chip muffins, cookies, fudge, and cakes. You delight in having Trent's friends grab a treat as they move in and out of his activities.

You eat little of what you prepare; your mission wholly is to remain active and to count yourself as a contributor. Four intense rounds of chemo have obliterated your ability to taste food. The act of eating lost its enjoyment for you as you entered year 4 of your war against cancer. In this, your sixth year of battle, you must force yourself to eat whenever you can. From your very first chemo treatment, vomiting has consistently been an outcome of eating. Now it is almost a guaranteed result. Short of vomiting are dry heaves, which are torturous to watch and obviously more traumatic physically and emotionally for you to endure. But endure you do for longer than anyone can comprehend.

Chemo notoriously causes side effects of constipation and diarrhea. You have dealt with these conditions all along. Constipation is the more constant enemy now. Irony prevailed when your body suffered from diarrhea and water retention simultaneously. Now cruelty reigns as your body retains everything. Even if you could enjoy food, psychologically the process of ingesting food proves problematic when you know that eliminating waste is so laborious. As part of your daily regimen of meds, vitamins, and holistic substances, you continue taking the diuretic Lasix for your edema; a stool softener, Surfak, for your constipation; as well as fiber tablets. This combination of treatments causes a comic and pathetic dissonance of physical reactions: you urinate as many as twenty times per day, but you only have a bowel movement once every five days, if you are lucky. Sometimes, you will sit on the toilet dripping urine or waiting for your bowels to move. You are sometimes literally in the bathroom more than any other room in the house.

Diuretics are extremely hard on kidneys. We talk as you sit on the toilet, feeling but not satisfying the urge to urinate. So often, the urine leaves your body reluctantly. A drip here and there, spits and spurts. Rarely do you manage a strong, steady stream. We wonder how badly your kidneys are being damaged. On the other hand, your edema is frightfully pronounced. Your right leg is literally more than twice the size of your left. Your shins and ankles feel as hard as any rock. The skin on your lower legs is sandpaper rough; the pallor, gray, the color of driftwood. When you do have a bowel movement, you have named it a pebble poop—an accurate descriptor. Ironic how long it takes to manufacture such small pieces of stool. In your mind, this inability to experience normal bodily functions stands as another defeat in your long, tiresome war. Struggling to eliminate waste is one more indignity in a string that you are becoming too weak to carry or abide much longer.

Which poison can you not live without? Which indignity can you not live with?

CHAPTER FORTY-FOUR

Brothers: I Carry All the Space You Once Occupied

In all our years together, you have always held your three brothers close in your consciousness and tight in your heart. You have always made sure that the Everidge men—Mike, Jeff, and Cary— literally and figuratively stepped as you have stepped by your side through life's pleasures and trials. They have always been such a striking part of your personality and an integral part of your bedrock optimism about life. Geography and gender have been irrelevant in their spiritual closeness to your nature and attitude, to your appreciation and enjoyment of life, to your decency and humanity.

Your brothers' love of people is your love of people. Your brothers' physical ruggedness is your physical ruggedness. Your brothers' instinct to defend victims of bullying or any form of oppression is your instinct to defend victims of bullying or any form of oppression. Your brothers' love of children is your love of children. Your brothers' athleticism is your athleticism. Your brothers' honest and realistic nature is your honest and realistic nature. Your brothers' strength of spirit and will is your strength of spirit and will.

The stories of your brothers' exploits have always been close to the surface of your daily life. You have spoken so admiringly, lovingly, and proudly about each of your brothers, reveling in their uniqueness and their commonality. You have always wanted all three of your brothers by your side in a fight and at life's most joyous moments.

Your brother Mike, the eldest, is a land steward in Indiana for the Nature Conservancy. As part of his responsibilities, he has been trained in managing and fighting wildland fires. He is a member of a twenty- man Indiana firefighting crew that responds to major wildland fires throughout the United States. He relishes opportunities to fight our country's most dangerous wildland fires alongside firefighters half his age, for which you are in awe. As a land steward, he is an expert in flora and fauna. So often you would casually look at a variety of tree or plant and think of your brother's knowledge of its history and characteristics. You have never stopped marveling at his uncommon goodness and decency and his abiding love for your home state of Indiana. When you talk to your brother Mike on the phone, your face lights up, and from across the room, I can feel the love you have for him.

Jeff, the middle brother, possesses a disarming sense of humor that never ceases to catch you off guard and causes you to laugh in the moment with abandon and for days afterward with sincere appreciation and joy. You have spoken of your high school years together about incidents when Jeff came to the defense of students who were being bullied and of how you always felt his shield of protection, despite his competitive nature that you had to learn to navigate. You have spoken often of Jeff's service in the army as a military policeman and his unparalleled work ethic in his role as a hands-on project manager for Woolf Steel, a structural steel fabrication company in Harrisburg, Pennsylvania.

Your younger brother, Cary, followed you after graduating from high school to Texas State University, the alma mater of Lyndon Baines Johnson, the thirty-sixth president of the United States, and George Strait, the country music star; and you love to tell stories of campus river rafting and sunbathing. Cary possesses a magnetic and magnanimous personality that makes everyone he encounters feel like family. He displays a special capacity to make ordinary moments extraordinary through his celebratory embrace of life. His easygoing nature disguises a piercing intelligence and wisdom that he has graciously used to gently influence your sons in an extraordinarily positive manner, for which you are eternally grateful. You have spoken so lovingly of Cary's skills as a businessman and his stellar ability to adapt to and overcome life's pressing challenges. With a background in medical equipment sales, he knows his way around hospitals and doctors with unique expertise.

Mike, Jeff, and Cary have added richness to your life that you value immeasurably. You hate cancer for how it has distanced you from having the strength to connect with all three of your brothers.

Your memories of spending time with your brothers occupy your thoughts as you carry on your fight. I have been fortunate to share some of those memories. During our trip to Indiana when you seemed to have cancer on the ropes, we spent two lovely days with Mike and his lovely wife Sharon, getting caught up on your home state, playing board games, and discussing children and the world.

Before you were diagnosed with cancer, we spent several memorable New Years' holiday seasons with Jeff, his gracious wife, Chrissy, and their sons Zachery and Luke in Pennsylvania, visiting Amish country, sitting around a cozy fire, playing the card game Hearts, and watching our kids play together.

Again, before cancer settled claim to you, we enjoyed Cary's generous sense of humor, his warmly encompassing spirit, and his gourmet culinary skills, able to transform venison into bites of paradise. Cary's lovely wife, Tammye, has always been your champion cheerleader.

You have made indelibly real the experiences with your family that I do not share from your telling and reliving to make me feel I actually was part of them.

You hold on to all your memories with ferocious intensity and love. You fight cancer partly to make your brothers proud of you and to honor all the love they have given you.

Your voice echoes within walls
Separating real from imagined;
Your voice resurrects hope within loss,
Communing divergent paths, holy and profane;
Your fingers intertwine memory and dream;
I can almost touch your tenderness.

I study the sky's hues of gifted pink
And seek other signs of eternal promise:
An owl's voice lighting the dark,
A fleeting image of limbs resurgent,
A whisper replenishing time's eroded promise,
A look borrowing from future emptiness.

I carry all the space you once occupied
And fill it with tribute welded by grief.

CHAPTER FORTY-FIVE

Strength Departs

A day comes when you can no longer bear the burden of cooking. Getting to the kitchen imposes too much of a strain on your weakening body. Pulling pots, pans, and utensils from the cabinets and drawers becomes too overwhelming. The look on your face betrays the defeat you feel. A demarcation line that I sense you will not return from occurred on a day when you simply tried to remove from the refrigerator a dish of chicken and potatoes that you wanted to snack from. You dropped the tray on your foot and the floor. Your arms lacked the strength to hold it steady. The ceramic dish cracked, but only after bruising your already swollen foot.

Luckily, I was home and able to get you back to your bed and clean up the mess. Once in bed, your countenance, which you could not hide, revealed the line between wanting to continue fighting and feeling the urge to succumb to cancer's invincibility. Your nature resisted giving in; it always had from the day you learned cancer had selected you for a fight. Reality, in the form of evidence that basic, independent day- to-day functioning was growing impossible, seemed to be demanding acknowledgment.

A day comes when you take a terrible fall in our laundry room. I am home and hear a frightening thud and then a cry of pain. I rush to the sound with the vibration of the thud still in my ears. I find you slumped between a wall and our washing machine. You are cursing the carpet that you caught your edematous foot on. You are calm yet clearly angry. "I am just like your mom. I cannot lift my feet above the throw rugs. What am I going to do?" We both know the significance of your question has nothing to do with rugs. But our only answer to your question is to pick up the few throw rugs we have throughout the house, mainly in the bathrooms. You were in the midst of doing laundry, a simple chore that remained a source of pride and usefulness for you. Even without a rug to contend with, you knew your days of doing laundry were coming to an end.

Days when I come home from work to find you planted on the sofa without the strength to stand up with your own leg strength are becoming more frequent. Your left leg is too emaciated to be of much use, and your right leg is so heavy with water retention that you cannot lift or maneuver it. For over six years, you have fought cancer with a streak of independence that has astonished your family, friends, nurses, doctors, and acquaintances around town in the bank and grocery store. You have been a source of inspiration to everyone who knows you and witnesses your positive attitude, your luminescent smile, your emotional grace, and your physical resolve.

You and I both know that your streak of defiant independence is coming to an end. I refrain from trying to convince you otherwise. Doing so seems disrespectful and lacking in integrity. Instead, I try to hold you with all the conviction that I possess. I try to be present when I am present. I try to convey how much I love you with every gesture, posture, and touch.

CHAPTER FORTY-SIX

Straw Thieves

Bell's palsy has dissuaded you from any desire to socialize or even venture out into the external world. The mere thought of going into a restaurant causes you great anguish. The brutal truth is that you are a fifty-year-old woman who cannot drink without a straw. You are mortified every time you squeeze your lips together and wedge a straw into your mouth to suck a bit of water or Coke or coffee. We strictly access the Starbucks drive-through on days when you feel emotionally strong enough to slurp your coffee through a straw. Putting food into your mouth requires planning and coordination. You must tilt your head to one side to keep food from falling out. You must only take childlike morsels, and chewing is drawn out and taxing. Biting your cheek is all too easy, as one side of your face is paralyzed. Overusing the other side and keeping food from the paralyzed side increase the chances of biting cheek, lips, or tongue. If food slides to the nonfunctioning side, you cannot always feel it, and thus biting yourself becomes likely. Taking a bite out of a sandwich has become absurdly out of the question.

At home, you use only two glasses. One is an extra-large Indianapolis Colts glass (you are forever loyal to your home state of Indiana), which I keep filled with water or Coke. The other is a cancer survivor glass with its own lid and reusable plastic straw. You were given the survivor glass, in the shade of lavender, the symbolic cancer survivor color, at a Relay for Life event in our home city of Tehachapi.

Straws have become a lifeline for you. To help you through your undignified ordeal of drinking, I have become a straw thief. I go into Starbucks or McDonald's, order coffee for me and unsweetened iced tea for you, and load up on straws. You sit in the car like a criminal lookout, anxiously awaiting my return to see how much "loot" I have escaped with. You stuff our contraband in the glove box as I hit the accelerator, pretending to flee invisible authorities in hot pursuit of the "straw bandits."

Cancer has taken quite a lot from both of us, you especially, but not our sense of humor.

Your food of choice has become fruit cocktail cups. The choice is a defensive one. These obviously require no preparation; the pieces of fruit are the right size for your impaired mouth. Little chewing is needed, reducing the chances you will bite yourself. The sweetness pleases your diminished taste buds. The only negative is that, as with straws, you feel childlike eating an item usually associated with children. I try to overlook the fact that you must carefully ingest no more than two pieces of the fruit at a time in order to minimize the chances of spillage or self-harm.

CHAPTER FORTY-SEVEN

A Wheelchair

On one of our trips to the cancer center, during your fourth round of chemo in your sixth year of fighting cancer, you inform me as we park that you cannot make it into the lobby under your own power. You ask me to get you a wheelchair. I immediately take off to secure one of the chairs that are typically available in the lobby.

The cancer center is undergoing an expansion project. In the blistering Bakersfield summer heat, we navigate our way through a security fence, over dirt where the concrete has been excavated, and to the sign-in desk. I must hand you the clipboard from the counter, as you cannot reach it from the wheelchair. I don't like anything about seeing you in the chair and having to assist you in signing in. I worriedly slide the clipboard back on the counter and then slowly maneuver you through a network of waiting chairs, afraid I might run over someone's toes, and I nestle you in to the spot where we usually sit in the lobby while we wait to be called.

We are by a large window and TV monitor, usually tuned to a cable news channel, but on this occasion, it's broadcasting a cooking channel. You are pleased to be distracted by happy people cooking instead of the usual somber talking heads informing us of never-ending examples of human degradation. I am fighting back tears as I fully perceive you sitting in a wheelchair, your purse resting on your lap. This is the first time you have ever needed a wheelchair to move from car to lobby. You have made it clear that you want to remain in the chair when we are called in for your blood work and to see the doctor.

Your shoulders are barely visible above the back of the chair. You have your pink Polo baseball cap on, slightly askew. Wisps of straw-colored hair hang beneath the rim of the cap. Your knees fold inward, and your New Balance athletic shoes seem cemented to the footrests.

After a short interval, I wheel you in to a nurses' station for a blood draw. You have gone through this procedure so many times that it barely gets your attention. The only difference today is that you are in a wheelchair, and you choose to remain in the chair for your weight check. This is possible as the cancer center has the equipment for permanently disabled patients to remain in their chairs for all procedures, including weight checks. I push you and the chair onto a metal hydraulic pallet for the check.

The blood draw is always the same—a nurse freezes your port-a-cath located just below your collarbone and to the right of your sternum. This freezing dulls the pain slightly when the needle is pushed down into the port-a-cath. The nurses all have the same cadence, "One, two, three," just before the push. You never flinch; I always do. I wheel you back out to our same spot in the waiting room to await the oncologist's call. I am getting better at maneuvering the wheelchair, which troubles me. I don't want to get better; I never want to have to push you in it again.

Your oncologist's nurse calls you within a few minutes and takes over the duty of pushing you in the chair. When your oncologist enters the exam room, he is shocked to see you in the chair. "What's this?" he asks.

You are calm, resigned. "I'm losing so much strength that it's harder and harder for me to walk."

With an undisguised edge to my voice, I interject, "Since we started a fourth round of chemo, Darlene has not been the same. She has been hit extremely hard by this latest treatment. I've never seen her hit so hard before. This is new and scary."

Your doctor is a bit defensive. "We only gave her a partial dose of what I prescribed. Sixty percent. Her body should not be reacting to that small a dosage this way."

I also point out that along your neckline are several lumps in various sizes, protruding visibly and annoyingly. The doctor feels them, then he asserts that we'll surely see them shrink with further chemo treatments.

After checking your blood work, the white and red blood cell levels are dangerously low. A blood transfusion is ordered. Another blood draw is necessary, and we will return tomorrow for the transfusion.

You have withstood multiple transfusions over the last two years. Usually we must go to the emergency room at Memorial Hospital in Bakersfield in order to get a transfusion. We are both relieved to know we will be spared that arduous ordeal on this occasion.

Getting you out of the wheelchair and into the car causes you understandable stress. You are not accustomed to wheelchairs and their machinations. You are fearful of a fall that will result in fractures. I have learned how to apply the brake so the chair will not slide or turn during the transfer. I have also learned how to pop off the footrests, giving you more unencumbered area to stand in once you are out of the chair. You are panicking that you cannot push yourself up and out of the chair on your own. I assure you that I can help. I stand directly in front of you, my feet straddling the width of the chair. I grab you around your torso and lift you to your feet. You do not have to push at all. You are surprised and grateful how easy the process turned out to be. I am dying inside and fighting back tears.

At home, I grab a beer and hide for a few minutes in the bathroom. Images of your agile feet bounding up and down subway steps in New York City flood my imagination. I see your long strides weaving in and out of pedestrians in Midtown Manhattan. You have no trouble keeping up with John-Michael's twenty-four-year-old cancer-free legs or Trent's sixteen-year-old cancer-free legs or my fifty-eight-year-old cancer-free legs. The beer helps me cut my tears; I don't want to cut the inspiring images of your physical strength and agility during our NYC trip; I cannot remove the sight of you looking so helpless in the wheelchair.

CHAPTER FORTY-EIGHT

Holding On and Letting Go

Watching you struggle to take a simple shower is nearly unbearable. I write that sentence in shame, for if your struggle is nearly unbearable to me, the witness, what must it be for you, the actor?

I want desperately to help, but little I offer to do eases your misery.

Our shower is a three-foot-by-three-foot square. You must step over a three-inch lip to enter. You worry about falling, as your edema-enlarged right leg and foot are becoming enormously arduous for you to lift or maneuver. I help you in and then stay close by in case you need assistance. I try not to hover, worried that I will make you feel even more helpless than you already feel.

For you, the pleasure of a shower is long gone. The process is purely functional and hygienic. The process has also devolved into an exhausting ordeal that leaves you utterly spent and demoralized.

I help you dry your lower body, as bending down threatens your balance and increases the likelihood of a fall. I cannot help but notice how you view your reflection in the mirror. The pain registering in your eyes is unmistakable and heartbreaking.

Your upper body seems to be closing in on itself. Your collarbone juts so unnaturally that it evokes Holocaust images of emaciated prisoners. The bones in your shoulder seem displaced; such is the extent to which they bulge. Your biceps are as thin as your wrists.

Your skeleton and musculature, what is left of them, can no longer support your implants. The scarring across both breasts, once a major concern, has healed nicely, but now this matters not at all.

Your spine seems ready to erupt from your flesh; your scapulae jut like fins on bygone-era Cadillacs.

Occasionally, our eyes meet in the mirror, and we are left speechless.

On another day, we try putting a chair in the shower so you can be free of the tiresome effort to stand while you wash yourself. This tactic proves too cumbersome. Our shower is not quite large enough for even a small chair. You cannot maneuver to wash all areas of your body.

On yet another day, we try a bath. We have an extra large and deep tub. Washing yourself proves easier than in the shower. The problem is that once in, we cannot get you out. The tub is too deep, and your legs and arms are too weak. I have to lift you as "dead weight" to extract you. The trauma of feeling trapped is too much to risk again, even knowing that I can get you out on my own without you having to do anything.

I can no longer in good conscience ask or expect you to continue suffering or sacrificing for my benefit. Your journey of fighting cancer is progressing beyond where I can follow and be of any help. At what point do I become a nuisance or interference, another milestone that you must pass with deep aggravation and grievance? Yet how does one let go?

How do I become an enemy of my own heart? For your sake, I must find a way. If I love you, I owe you such loyalty.

I must clear your way to the edge of earthly pain,
Cut a path through snarling, foolish deterrence and false hope,
Leave you where you can say goodbye in humble lasting triumph
To the disease that has raped and ravaged without pause.

I can no more allow you to languish long past your due.
What color are the stars up close? Which one may I touch first?
And the voices of school kids and angels call out
Answers to make you smile and forget and go home.

CHAPTER FORTY-NINE

A Mother Tried and True

Somehow, the width of your single-size hospital bed accommodates both you and our youngest son, Trent, who is six feet four inches tall. The length of the bed is another matter. His legs extend far beyond the bottom edge; his feet are like twin rudders rising out of the imaginary sea.

Your heads rest together, and your bodies become one as you will yourself to whisper hard words, a mark of your maternal love, strength, and courage—words that Trent is mature enough to hear and comprehend at the tender age of sixteen. I try to disappear in the background as emotional grenades explode in my mind in quiet succession; these grenades of raw fear and doom will reverberate in my psyche forever.

So often over the last few months, I have witnessed this display of your raw force of will to prepare your son for life without his mother. I am in awe of your resolve, tenacity, and wisdom. I am mystified by the strength you muster to tenderly infuse spiritual amniotic fluid into your son's lifeblood—an urgent symbiosis never more necessary and effectively delivered.

I slip away to the recesses of our house in some half-assed Hemingway impersonation, trying to be strong in all the weak places, failing miserably, sipping beer to dull the sting of life's most exposed, jagged edge.

I am humbled by your motherhood, which is now and which will remain eternally cancer-free.

In your fifth year of fighting cancer, you decided that we should purchase a hospital bed. We had talked about it several times, and you had finally admitted that it would be appropriate. The purchase represented an admission that your disease was winning, and you were understandably reluctant to give in to that notion.

You had only slept in our bedroom on a few occasions. Sometimes, you would arrange on your side of the bed a special back-support cushion with armrests, and I would stretch out next to you. The cushion would allow you to sit upright and recline slightly. You could read, pay bills, write note and birthday cards to family and friends, text, and talk on the phone. The pain in your back from the cancer and arthritis caused by chemo would not allow you to lie flat. On these occasions, you rarely fell asleep. If you did doze off, it would only be for a few minutes. You would wake me and say that you were moving out to the living room to sit on the sofa. I always followed you and set up a pallet on the floor. You would put the TV on for distraction from the pain, and I would eventually fall asleep. Sometimes you slept, and often you endured intense pain relieved inadequately by morphine and pain patches.

We followed this routine for years. We reached a point when you stopped using our bed completely. I stopped using it as well. I kept pillows and blankets in our living room and made my pallet on the floor nightly. We kept bedding for you to use on our sofa.

The hospital bed was a Craftmatic, single width and extra long to accommodate your five feet nine inches height. We both dreaded and anticipated the bed's arrival date. When that day arrived, we adjusted the furniture in our living room to accommodate the bed. You refused to be isolated in a bedroom and away from Trent, John-Michael (when he was home from college), or me. The two young men who delivered the bed set it up within minutes and gave us a lesson on how to use the remote control to adjust the mattress into various positions. We appreciated their professionalism and politeness. It eased our emotional distress at having such an obtrusive sign of your diminishing physical condition established in the heart of our home.

For a few moments, we let ourselves be distracted by the multiple ways the bed's mattress could be adjusted. We could elevate the bottom of the mattress, and we could move the top of the mattress into various states of recline. Of course, the mattress could be kept perfectly flat, but we knew it would never be in that position. The mattress even had a massage feature; Trent loved that, but you found it to be weird and ticklish.

When the two young men had departed, we played with the remote for a few minutes. You had bought sheets and a bedspread, and we took forced delight in making up the new addition to our loving room. After we had the bed set exactly where you wanted it and sheets, pillows, and bedspread were perfectly placed, you looked at me and calmly stated, "You know I'm going to die in this bed."

I dismissed your statement with foolish bravado. "Sweetheart, you're not dying anywhere. This bed is just to help you fall asleep. You can raise the bed to ease the pain in your back, watch TV, and get some much-needed sleep."

Your eyes let me know that you found my denial of reality embarrassing.

CHAPTER FIFTY

Fears and Prayers

I pray that you do not perceive me to be as helpless as I feel. I pray that I am not as helpless as I fear myself to be. Moments when you ask me softly to hold you and will a transfer of healing energy into your body offer an all-too-brief respite from the onslaught you endure. These moments have seared my soul in a way that nothing else in life has. We are one—a symmetrical drop of water delicately balanced between waiting and urging, between sorrow and salvation, between hope and acceptance.

My soul cries out to know if we are rising or falling, or if these are one and the same. I secretly pray that the cancer will leave your body and enter mine. This is not an act of courage or nobility; it is an act of panic, fear, and desperation. I know that if I lose you, I will also lose myself. So what on the surface appears to be selfless turns out in deeper inspection to be selfish. Still, these moments when we hold each other cannot last long enough, yet they are among the few experiences in my life that have lasting power.

I know that you are in the process of leaving. How could you not want to leave, need to leave, after all that you have withstood? You sleep more than you ever have; your time awake is preoccupied with matters that I cannot understand or be a part of. I am tethered to the physical world that we used to share, and you are transitioning to a metaphysical world that is not ready to welcome me.

In so many ways, you have already left. I know that I must find the grace to accept your leaving, to not take it personally, to not feel victimized by it, to respect God's plan. Your cancer is not about me; it never was about me.

How humiliating to recall moments when I felt inconvenienced by it. When I anguished over whether to stay home or go to work. When I failed to appreciate the pain you endured waiting for me to get home from work, to finish foolish errands such as buying toothpaste or socks.

I am starting to be haunted by the man I was before you came into my life. That man I said goodbye to long ago. Without your continued help, can I continue to be the man you have helped me to become? I must put aside these questions. You still have fighting to do. I must fight with you every step of the way. This is the most important thing I have ever done. I must not become helpless to you. I must not allow my fear to render me helpless. I must stay in step with you as far as I am able to.

CHAPTER FIFTY-ONE

Self-Deception and Self-Deception No More

Looking back, thinking that I was going through your journey of fighting cancer, step for step with you, seems humiliatingly presumptuous and naive. I have a sense, too late, of how lonely you must have felt, of how alone you must have felt, of how hours must have mocked you with ponderous indifference, while I continued to engage, albeit with less enthusiasm, in an external world that no longer welcomed you. And now my external world is what remains, and it mocks me with the same ponderous indifference.

Walls and floors had become such an enemy to you, and now they are my enemy. You were constrained against all hope and escape. How they inched closer to your heart every day. At least I could depart and benefit from the distraction of commuting, working, and selfishly recovering from daily stresses.

You had become an immobile target, and thus all the more vulnerable. You had no choice but to hunker down in your hospital bed, your wheelchair, and your port-a-potty. And now I hunker down in my loss, my grief, and my whole-scale emotional destruction.

I thought I understood what was happening to you and how you felt, but I was only fooling myself. Now I fool myself no longer, and I understand so much more.

To you on the other side I send my fervent prayers that somehow you know that I know better and deeper and more profoundly what you endured and how you endured.

CHAPTER FIFTY-TWO

Chicago

I am drawn to an interlude in your fifth year of battle. You rightly leveled against me a charge that I was not recognizing how dire your situation truly was, and you asked me to take a leave from my work to support you more consistently. I buried my wounded pride, took a leave, and set about arranging for a second opinion about your condition and treatment.

We ended up going to Chicago for two weeks, where you were able to receive a fresh diagnosis. The outcome of the fresh diagnosis ironically ended up being more chemo, framed in a different context, less about estrogen causation and more about consequence, specifically the advance of cancer into your bones and lungs.

Psychologically and spiritually, you were crushed by the harsh reality that chemo remained the chief answer to cancer's onslaught. We changed doctors, facilities, philosophies, office furniture, and geography, but the treatment stayed true in all its single-minded inglorious lethality.

During this interlude, what remains essential to your story is how you triumphed over the crushing lie that chemo was your rightful medical ally. Neither one of us had ever been to Chicago, so we decided to see as much of the city as we could. Later, we learned that you were functioning somehow with only 25 percent breathing capacity in one lung. The other lung was at 50 percent capacity. Diminished lung capacity stopped you not at all. We traveled from the suburbs to the inner city by train. We sat in the quiet car and prayed, our hands interlocked and our heads pressed together, asking humbly for divine help, committing ourselves to positive thinking and renewing our "never say die" oath. We got off the train at Union Station and walked to the famous Magnificent Mile shopping district, a trek through forty-degree temperatures of about two miles. We crossed the Michigan Avenue Bridge countless times for the experience of it. So taken were we by the Michigan River, the skyscrapers, the people, the crisp air, the rush of all manner of vehicles.

We walked up and down Michigan Avenue, slipping in and out of stores, weaving in and out of pedestrians with cancer-free ease. We took in all the store windows like kids at old-fashioned candy counters; we searched for just the right elegant restaurant with a piano bar and exquisite Italian fare. On the next day, we walked from Union Station to the Navy Pier, nearly two and a half miles, repeating our sightseeing of city life, but this time with a majestic view of Lake Michigan. Diminished lung capacity damned by your will to irrelevance.

How I long desperately for you to relive those moments of quiet and humble victory. How I long to relive them with you. For as long as I live, I will never witness your brand of heroism again, nor do I care to.

CHAPTER FIFTY-THREE

Takeaways

I am embarrassed to remember how I reacted when your doctor informed you that round 4 of chemo was necessary, as the cancer had spread to your lungs and liver and was threatening your kidneys.

"You've done chemo before, you are a veteran. You know what to expect. You've proved you are strong enough to withstand it, to survive it. We can do this." How utterly presumptuous of me to use the pronoun *we* and to tell you what your capabilities were. The past is so humiliating.

You had soldiered on for more than six years—years of having your life taken away bit by bit: work, face-to-face connections with your family and friends, interactions with the surprises and stresses of daily life, the ability to function physically, the enjoyment of preparing and consuming food, the desire to seize a moment and exhibit unfettered passion and zaniness, the power to help your youngest son with schoolwork, the dominant personality needed to influence and guide your oldest son through life's challenges. And on and on the stealing of your life continued unabated.

Your consumption of food became limited to fruit cups, juice bars, soup, and an occasional sliver of chicken. Even with such a reduced diet, you still vomited frequently, experienced dry heaves, and had major trouble urinating and moving your bowels.

It was no longer possible to go for a walk. No longer possible to meet your friends for lunch. No longer possible to jump in the car and whimsically drive to a shopping mall and spend money on loved ones and yourself. No longer possible to push a grocery cart up and down aisles, looking for deals or just the right box of crackers. No longer possible to retrieve a paint can from the garage and touch up a few spots of wear or chipping. No longer possible to create posters that you took so much pride in for the next Relay for Life event. No longer possible to drop letters in the mail, open our mailbox, and yank out the stack of catalogues and bills, or buy seasonal stamps that delighted your senses beyond reason. You were no longer able to feel the rain on your face and stomp through puddles, reliving childhood. No longer able to form a snowball and plunk me in the chest, evoking a look of feigned shock on my face then zigzagging down the driveway to escape my retaliation. No longer strong enough to hold a plate or retrieve from the refrigerator a carton of milk or plastic bottle of juice.

CHAPTER FIFTY-FOUR

Too Many Battlefronts

The language of the clinical diagnoses of your condition tells so little of the story you have lived.

> Malignant neoplasm of lower-outer quadrant of female breast—left Modified radical mastectomy
> Secondary malignant neoplasm of bone and bone marrow
> Unspecified vitamin D deficiency
> Other malaise and fatigue
> Nausea and vomiting

Translated into human life, these diagnoses have meant that for five years, you have been walking around without breasts or nipples. Yes, you have silicone implants, minus nipples, but the implants come with an expiration date, which you carry in your wallet like a library card. Maddeningly, the expiration dates do not match. Your left silicone- filled breast implant expires in August of 2015. Your right one expires in March of 2016. They will need to be replaced, like tires.

The cancer in the bones of your spine, pelvis, and extremities causes pain that sometimes cannot be eased by morphine, which you are prescribed to take in thirty-milligram tablets every four hours. Your pain laughed at the Valium and hydrocodone that you were initially prescribed. You have taken as many as eight morphine tablets in a two-hour period, to no avail. You routinely double your prescription to make it through the night when the pain intensifies.

Your oncologist has also prescribed Fentanyl pain patches, seventy- five micrograms in strength, which you may apply to your body every seventy-two hours. You are only supposed to wear one patch at a time. Sometimes, you have two or three patches in different places on your body, and still the pain rages on.

You and I have researched alternative treatments that do not conflict with your doctor's prescriptions. Consequently, you rub vitamin E oil, frankincense oil, and myrrh oil into the skin covering your breasts, back, hips, arms, legs, and feet. We apply these oils in extra generous amounts to the lateral scars that cross your breast implants. You believe in the healing properties of these oils, and we make regular trips to our local health store to make sure we are always well stocked.

The malignancy in your bone marrow means that you can no longer manufacture red and white blood cells naturally. Your platelet counts are also diminished. What this means is that you must have blood transfusions regularly. Also, you must inject white blood cells into your body. You have been taught how to do this on your own. Our refrigerator is loaded with boxes of hypodermic needles filled with white blood cells.

Despite the fact that you drink as much water as you are able to, your compromised immune system means that you frequently experience urinary tract infections. Sometimes, the over-the-counter medicine Azo suffices, but often you must be prescribed the antibiotic Cipro. You take IP6 tablets to strengthen your immune system.

Cancer and chemo have killed your appetite and ability to taste food. The combination of disease and treatment has also made it difficult for you to keep food in your system on those occasions when you are able to consume a bit of nourishment. You keep a trash receptacle by your side as you sit in your hospital bed. I cannot count the number of times I have watched you heave out of your system in violent spasms whatever you have managed to eat. I am helpless with a cool washcloth and physical support as your body wretches and writhes. The vomiting often brings you to your knees.

Nausea has been a constant companion for all the years that you have endured. Sometimes the mere aroma of food causes you inordinate distress. In your first two rounds of chemo, diarrhea became a regular occurrence. In your second two rounds of chemo, constipation has emerged as the problem. In response, you have added to your supplements fiber tablets and Surfak, a stool softener. You struggle to find a balance between unpleasant extremes.

Over the years you have adjusted your diet in various ways. You have eliminated sugar, red meat, dairy, and processed foods; you have increased your consumption of fruits and vegetables. You have now reached a phase in which cancer determines your diet. In the fifth and sixth year of battle, I estimate that you are consuming fewer than five hundred calories each day.

You counteract the vitamin D deficiency with a plethora of vitamin supplements and homeopathic substances, all of which you carry with you in an oversize tote bag throughout the house and in public. The bag is never out of reach; you have carried it with you at all times for nearly seven years. It contains D-3, B-6, B complex, C, E, magnesium, zinc, potassium, folic acid, iron, black raspberry, and Ubiquinol CoQH. It also contains your morphine tablets, as well as Extra Strength Tylenol.

Additionally, your medicine bag contains a diuretic called Lasix, which you take to reduce the edema that has enlarged your right leg to twice the size of your left. Lasix increases both the urge to urinate as well as the release of urine, albeit in frustratingly small spasms. Your bag also contains a drug called Letrozole, which has been prescribed for you as a postmenopausal patient because it inhibits your body's production of estrogen, which is thought to be a catalyst for your metastatic breast cancer.

If your medicine bag is out of your sight line, you become nervous and uncomfortable. The bag is far more important that anything you have ever carried in your purse. You are comfortable without your purse; you are never comfortable without your green medicine bag overflowing with plastic pill bottles.

Fatigue has been a major side effect of every chemo treatment you have received. During your first two rounds, spanning four years, you have maintained a robust attitude, demeanor, and posture during the actual treatment, which typically takes three to four hours and immediately afterward. As you sit in the recliner, you interact with your nurses as if you were engaged in a social setting. You ask about their lives and how long they have been working as oncology nurses. You interact with other patients when they seem open to your comments or questions. I outfit you with magazines, snacks, iced tea, and bills if you need to write out checks, which you enjoy. In fact, you have actually shown signs over your years of treatment of being energized by the chemo treatments. The fatigue, predictable, seriously sets in about twelve hours after you have arrived home. You then exhibit signs of being utterly exhausted for as long as a week after a treatment. The second, third, and fourth days are especially difficult, during which you have trouble adjusting your position on the sofa or in bed, and walking from one room to another becomes an extremely difficult and taxing chore. You have hours when lifting your head from a pillow without a marshaling of will and sometimes assistance proves almost impossible. But after a week, you are back to your jaunty self.

However, the third and fourth rounds of chemo in your fifth and sixth years of fighting cancer have affected you in a startlingly debilitating manner. During treatment, you remain passive, inert, disengaged from your surroundings. Your interactions with nurses are nearly nonexistent after the initial greeting. You are oblivious to other patients or to your surroundings. The cancer center is undergoing a major renovation, inside and out, which hardly catches your attention. Your body seems to almost disappear in the recesses of the recliner. Mostly, your eyes are closed. I can offer you little in the way of comforts or distractions. Sometimes you are unaware of the nurses changing your IV bags from antinausea medicine to the actual chemo drugs. You sleep, occasionally opening your eyes for a few moments, then close them again and drift off. At home you are immobile, detached, unaware of externals: noise, movement, entrances and exits by Trent or me. Hours pass and your body remains in the same position. You occasionally turn your head with extreme effort from one side to the other.

In looking at the printouts describing the chemo drugs you are having pumped into your system, I learn that one is known as Taxotere by its trade name and docetaxel in the generic form. It is used to treat metastatic breast cancer and lung cancer. The other chemo drug you are being given simultaneously is Paraplatin (trade name), or carboplatin (generic form). It is also prescribed for lung cancer. Although you are still classified as a breast cancer patient, the focus of your treatment has clearly shifted to your lungs and bones.

Your lungs have suffered drastically from cancer's invasion. Shortness of breath has become a new normal for you. You are walking less and less. When you do walk from one room to another, you must stop every few steps to steady yourself, catch your breath, and regain confidence that you can actually reach the kitchen or the bathroom. We must now take you to yet another doctor to have your lungs drained of fluid. The first time we did this, the doctor drained nearly two liters from your right lung. Your breathing capacity had been reduced to 35 percent of what is considered normal. Your doctor is surprised you can walk in such a state.

The procedure to have your lungs drained of fluid is called thoracentesis. Encircling the lungs is a double layer of membranes called the pleura. In lungs that are functioning properly, a little fluid in the pleura prevents the membranes from rubbing together when one breathes. When too much fluid accumulates in the pleura, the lungs are not able to inflate normally and breathing becomes difficult. This usually causes shortness of breath, and it can be very painful. Physical activity can be severely restricted. Simple walking can become arduous.

You sit up through the outpatient procedure. The doctor inserts a frightening long needle through your back, through your ribs, and into the pleura. The excess fluid is withdrawn through the needle and through tubing that empties into a ridiculously large plastic bottle. The fluid drips steadily for an hour. The dirty liquid drains and drains and drains.

Although the procedure is relatively simple, and the doctor is aided by computer technology that allows him to aim with pinpoint accuracy, a danger of your lung collapsing is ever present, accelerating your heart rate and increasing your stress level.

During the procedure, your eyes nearly stop blinking. You fix your gaze on me, and I know what you are thinking: You are being asked to fight on too many battlefronts at once. Cancer invades tissue, lungs, liver, and other areas and organs yet to be discovered, despite whatever combination of specific chemo drugs your oncologist prescribes. You must find a way to endure intense physical pain that your doctors can no longer manage or control. The edema in your right leg and foot seems permanent. Bell's palsy has laid a seemingly permanent claim to the left side of your face and left eye. Blood transfusions and white blood cell injections are now regular procedures, like filling up a car with fuel. Your body is becoming so weak that you can no longer lift yourself off the toilet or get yourself into bed without assistance.

If all this were not enough, you are now having trouble swallowing the barest amount of water or a few morsels of fruit. And we now have evidence from a scan that a suspicious mass is on the verge of reaching one of your kidneys.

CHAPTER FIFTY-FIVE

Verse

Rows of oaks
(Rows of woes):
A returning of bull elk
Early summer
As always,
Settling on the valley floor
Nestling deep
Within the sweeping blonde grass,
Oblivious to cars and admirers;
I almost forgot until a driver stopped

I look (not from my vantage point)
And then look away,
Knowing you will never look again
Knowing you would object
If I didn't look;
I force myself to look again
With meaning meagerly manufactured,
Looking for you, not me.

They rest regally while
I writhe in your absence

CHAPTER FIFTY-SIX

Your Time

I don't know if I am strong enough to write the last part of your nearly seven-year fight against cancer. I do know that I don't want to write it, even though telling your story makes me feel closer to you than I otherwise feel. The telling eases the pain I feel constantly in my heart. The telling lets me breathe a little more deeply, see a little more clearly. The telling reignites a desire to carry on in a meaningful way, honoring all the eternal values and principles that your life represented.

On Monday evening of September 28, 2015, you could not sustain your own weight under your own power in a fixed position. You could not walk without assistance, you could not breathe deeply, you could not swallow without difficulty, and you had virtually no appetite. Each of these realities had been gradual in its advancement, but with a suddenness that neither of us could absorb, each reached a pinnacle of intensity and undeniability that caught us off guard.

In the two weeks leading up to this juggernaut, your oncologist had referred us to consultations with two specialists. The first appointment was with a gastroenterologist to discuss possible intestinal investigations (upper GI, lower GI, colonoscopy) to determine precisely why you were having so much trouble eating. The doctor quickly judged that you were far too weak to endure any additional procedures at that time. The second referral was to an endocrinologist to discuss the possibility of having a stint inserted into the ureter to increase the productivity of one kidney, thus facilitating the easier evacuation of urine. A scan earlier in the month had detected a blockage, which was making it harder for your body to eliminate liquid waste. After studying the results of your scan, the endocrinologist explained that most likely cancer cells were pressing on your ureter, much like a car tire would press on a water hose that it had run over, thus restricting the flow of water, in your situation, urine. However, your other kidney seemed to be compensating for this restriction, meaning that surgery was not essential. The doctor explained that the procedure was relatively simple, much like having a catheter inserted, only going much deeper with the device, requiring anesthesia but no incision. He adamantly stated that he would only perform the procedure if your oncologist insisted that it was necessary for his treatment of your cancer. He also ascertained that you were far too weak to endure any additional procedures unless they were determined to be lifesaving.

During both of these consultations, you were in a wheelchair, unable to walk on your own. You were so weak that you could not get yourself out of or into the wheelchair without major help. While we were waiting to see the endocrinologist, you needed to use the restroom. I wheeled you in to the thankfully large room and helped you move from the wheelchair to the toilet. I then exited the room to give you privacy. Stupidly, I locked the door on my way out. I will never know how you managed to get yourself off the toilet and back into the wheelchair. We were speaking through the locked door as you dealt with my foolishness.

In our laymen minds, the referrals by your oncologist to the specialists were gratuitous. Getting you to these appointments taxed you beyond reason. The referral to the gastroenterologist was scheduled in the late afternoon after you had had a blood transfusion (two liters) at the cancer center, which was an exhausting all-day process. Yet somehow you soldiered through with Herculean fortitude and strength. After both consultations, we shared and regretted our common assessment that both doctors showed facial expressions that said, "Dear lady, why are you here? You should be home in bed, resting to regain physical strength." To that juncture in your interminable battle, cancer had laid you as low physically as I had ever witnessed.

Simply seeing you in the wheelchair broke my heart beyond repair. Assuring you that we could safely get you into and out of our vehicle proved as difficult as physically managing the transfers. Watching your world shrink ever more caused an emotional wrenching and retching that remains unrecoverable.

I tried to joke, and you tried to go along. Pushing you in the chair, I would exaggerate turns and weave left and right for no reason other than to make you laugh. But it was a false laugh—an effort on your part to mercifully acknowledge my attempts to be lighthearted. In reality, at the wretched advances cancer had achieved, both our hearts were shattered and were falling to depths irretrievable by our comprehension or coping mechanisms.

Any retelling of our final reckoning of how we told each other what it all meant and would forever mean in the depths of loss and separation would be hopelessly meager and forlorn. You sat in your hospital bed, immobile, unable to swallow, too weak to draw water through a straw. I sobbed and blew my nose and expressed my devotion. I tried to explain my gratitude for how you elevated every particle of my being with your love, your towering and commanding strength, your uncompromising embrace of all my faults and weaknesses. Your blood was settling; your lungs were shutting down. Your soul was preparing to depart.

We had no need to declare our love for each other. Of that no doubt could ever be part of the equation. You let me know that as a caregiver, I had helped you more than anyone else could have. That you would not have wanted to endure the path you had been on for the last seven years with anyone but me. That you knew how I longed to trade places with you if only God would allow it. That you would never have wanted God to allow such a trade.

I tried to convey how you had saved me from a meaningless life. That you had taught me what it means to love life; to be grateful for God's gifts; to be a giving person; to be without ego, without narcissism, without presumption. That you had taught me to release anger and acquire grace. That you were my world, my longing, my peace. That I wanted nothing more of this world than to oxygenate your cells and push your blood through your body. Short of that, that I wanted to accompany your soul as far as God would allow.

Your eyes belied the question that you whispered only once: "Am I dying?"

Nothing left to do but go to the hospital.

The only personal items of importance you wanted to take with you to the hospital were placed in a keepsake cardboard box. The small box was adorned with a muted sunflower. Inside you placed a ceramic heart that your youngest son had made for you in 2010, a note from your oldest son declaring his love for you, a note from me expressing my belief that you had saved me from a meaningless life, a poem written to you by your unofficial adopted daughter, and from a faraway Baptist church, a mystery gift that symbolized God's warmth and love. In your purse, you had a partial, early draft of this book. Of course, we brought your oversize bag of medications and vitamins.

We had been to the emergency room of our local hospital so often that the admitting staff knew your condition and efficiently processed you into a private room. We were long past the point of being frustrated by the cumbersome and inconvenient method of having you admitted to the hospital. In a more idealized world, your oncologist would have been able to make a phone call, enabling us to bypass the emergency room experience. That not being the case, we navigated on our own. The hospital staff demonstrated as much compassion and efficiency as the chaotic and highly pressured emergency room milieu would permit. Once we got you into a bed with warm blankets, little else mattered. Our youngest son and I did our best to keep you comfortable and lighthearted. You seemed reassured by the attention of our nurse and doctor.

Blood transfusions were ordered, your bedsores were examined, and the doctor urged you to eat as much as you could and drink Ensure until you could drink it no more.

We had to wait on a possible admittance, a familiar procedure that we knew all too well.

Our nurse took a photo of the bedsores that surrounded your anus. In an unforeseeable and awkward moment, she showed me the photo and told me that you had a "lovely butt." I'm sure my face lost all color, and I was too taken aback to respond. Sensing my discomfort, the nurse clarified that what she meant was that whatever we were doing to combat her bedsores was working. I explained that our routine was to apply generous amounts of Neosporin multiple times per day and to make sure that you shifted your weight with the aid of pillows as you lay in your hospital bed. The nurse applauded our efforts as I uncomfortably viewed the photo.

By about 6:00 p.m. that evening, you had been admitted to the hospital. We had spent nearly twelve hours in the small emergency room. In the afternoon, you needed to have a bowel movement, something we were ecstatic about since you had not had one for about five days. The restroom was across the hallway. You insisted on walking rather than using your wheelchair. This small act of defiance and determination to function normally evidenced your overall attitude to cancer: "I will fight you to whatever eternal gates await me."

In the hospital room, several doctors visited you. They ordered endless bottles of Ensure, body scans, and treatment for your edema. We laughed at the questions and discussions about your edema. For more than a year, no one had been able to affect it to any significant degree. You stared derisively at the doctor as he ordered your legs to be elevated and the leg compression machine to be hooked up. The scans to determine the state of your lungs and other vital organs would commence later that night and continue the following morning. Solid food was ordered, although I knew you had no appetite and would do little more than push it aside. You could barely get down a sip of

Ensure. The doctors just didn't understand how hard it had become for you to swallow and keep down food.

When only the two of us were in the room, I could not help but see that you were mostly oblivious to the rush of activity around you. You concentrated on finding a comfortable position in bed and making sure you had warm blankets. You were weak to the point that I had to reposition your body to find not a happy spot but at least an endurable one. Without saying anything, I knew you wanted the doctors to leave you alone.

We held our composure by making only fleeting eye contact. Trent distracted himself by wheeling adroitly around your room in the wheelchair. You laughed silently at his antics.

After leaving you in a state of utter fatigue to hopefully get some sleep, Trent and I drove home to make sure he was ready for school the next morning. He slept most of the way home, and I fought back thoughts and tears.

Once home, Trent followed me down our hallway and asked, "Is Mom going to die?" This was the first time he had ever posed the direct question. We sat on the couch, and I answered his question with as much delicacy as I could muster. "You have watched your mother fight cancer with all her strength and willpower. I don't know if she is going to die, but she is getting close to being finished with her battle. The cancer isn't going to give up. Your mom isn't going to give up either, but she is getting tired. I'm not sure how much longer she can fight."

Trent sat quietly composed through my answer, and then we cried together, held each other, and eventually went to bed. The house had become extraordinarily dark, quiet, and empty. I could not bear to look at your hospital bed, the covers reckless and wanting.

I am ambivalent about the treatment you received during your last day of life. The hospital staff aggressively responded to your weakened condition. You had multiple tests, X-rays, and scans. You were fed constantly and urged to drink as much Ensure as you could stomach. A catheter was inserted to monitor the functioning of your kidneys. Your legs were elevated and compressed by machine to prevent clotting.

You were passively enduring all the attention and treatment and testing. Your youngest brother was flying in from Houston, and you were not anxious for him to see you in such a weakened condition. With such a look of consternation, you asked me why he was coming to see you; I almost cried. The last time he had seen you was two years ago when you looked so healthy that people could only look in disbelief when they found out you were battling cancer. During that visit with Jeff, we had bowled, attended a county fair, and generally acted with reckless frivolity and silliness. Now, I could only say he was coming to be by your side out of love and respect. You made it clear that your preference was for him to stay away. You simply did not want anyone to see you in such a helpless state.

I talked with one of the hospital doctors who was treating you. We discussed the option of putting you in hospice care. The dilemma was over the issue of ceasing all treatment of your cancer. We sat in a hospital waiting room in semidarkness. I could not have imagined a more sterile, inhospitable environment in which to have such a monumentally important and gut-wrenching discussion.

I hadn't realized that hospice care would effectively stop all efforts to fight your cancer and concentrate strictly on controlling your pain and keeping you comfortable. The doctor was professional and helpful, but I wanted to be having this conversation with your oncologist instead. I made a decision to contact hospice only to initiate a visit from one of its representatives to assess your condition and readiness for such care. I desperately needed to consult with your oncologist. I called the cancer center to leave a message about your situation and my need to speak with him.

Everything was happening so quickly.

Your brother Cary arrived in the midafternoon and could not have been more loving to you. He managed in your presence to control his emotions, but outside of your hospital room, he and I broke down and shared our sadness and sense of foreboding gloom.

Your brother's wife, Tammye, and your brother Jeff were set to arrive the following day. Again, you were uncomfortable with more family members coming to see you in such a dire condition. In light of your pained, distressed countenance, I could only repeat softly, almost apologetically, how much people loved you.

I accompanied you to one of your body scans, which had been ordered to determine what was happening with your major organs. The doctors were ready to order intravenous nutrition since you were wholly without an appetite, could swallow only with extreme difficulty, and could barely keep solid food down. During the scan, you had to lie flat, something you never did except for a procedure. The physical pain for you was beyond the reach of morphine and pain patches. Your body would simply not cooperate with the requirements of the procedure, resulting in a major anxiety attack. I intervened and tried to calm you and help you through the scan. I gave you a pep talk, reminding you of how many times before you had endured such a procedure. What a naive blowhard I acted. I will forever regret urging you to get through the scan. I should have shut the whole operation down and taken you back to your room. The attendants ironically thanked me for "helping." Had you been stronger, you would have implored me rightfully to get you out of the scanning room immediately. The attendants got their pictures, lot of good it did you. I was still in a "fighting" mode, stupidly blind to the fact that you were "beyond" fighting.

Back in your private room, you looked somewhat relieved to be in bed, but the fatigue registering in your face had a permanence that scared me to my core. Your eyes were becoming more and more detached from whatever you were viewing. I saw in your eyes what I interpreted as a desire to be gone from your suffering. I could not blame you. I could not will you to continue fighting against what now seemed to be in your own estimation an insurmountable enemy. You looked with disdain at the nurses who brought you more bottles of Ensure. You looked with disinterest at the hapless Los Angeles Angels as their chances of securing a playoff birth fizzled.

I am not sure how we passed the evening hours. You slipped in and out of wakefulness. Your rest, a misnomer to call it that, was anything but easy and restorative. Your breathing was labored; your restlessness in bed, heartbreaking. Your hospital gown annoyed you, yet you were indifferent to the catheter that was yielding precious little urine. A nurse expressed dismay that the container dangling from the bed contained such a small amount of urine. She urged me to urge you to drink more. She outlined more tests scheduled for tomorrow.

A dear friend of yours whom you taught with and her husband, Kris and Alex Zonn, arrived to visit you. Your brother Cary, Trent, and I gave them time alone with you, and we went to the hospital cafeteria for a bite to eat.

On our way back to your room, we ran into Kris and Alex outside an elevator. They were both struggling to hold back their tears. Kris told me that you had informed her that your time was coming much sooner than you ever thought it would. Her husband looked at me with the deepest sadness and dejection I had ever seen in a human face. We hugged, and they slowly made their brokenhearted way out of the hospital. The three of us made our brokenhearted way back to your room.

At about 11:00 p.m., you were requesting time to sleep. You urged us to leave and get some rest. Trent hugged you and told you he loved you. He would see your tomorrow. After I kissed you on the forehead, both cheeks, and chin, a ritual we began when your Bell's palsy made it difficult for you to kiss with your lips, you winked at me as if to say you had things under control and everything would be all right. To your brother Cary, you said, "Being your sister has been my privilege."

These were the last words I would ever hear you speak, and this was the last time I would see you alive.

Cary drove to his hotel room, and Trent and I drove home. Two hours later, the phone rang, and a nurse said I needed to come to the hospital immediately. I woke Trent, and he said he wanted to return with me.

In the car on our way back to the hospital, my cell phone rang. It was about 2:30 a.m. the first day of October 2015. The nurse informed me that you had had a cardiac episode, and without life support, you were not going to survive. I had to instruct the doctor how to proceed. Your advanced health care directive made it clear that you did not want to be put on life support. That document did not make my decision any easier. I still had to utter the words. I said that CPR was okay but no to placing you on life-support machines. The nurse made it clear that in that case, you would die. I know that the nurse only wanted me to understand the consequences of what I was saying. She wanted confirmation of what I had said so there would be no misunderstanding. I asked her to wait, and I consulted with Trent. At sixteen years of age, he knew the situation from my side of the conversation. He told me that I was making the right decision.

I returned to the nurse and confirmed my decision. I have never felt more like a failure and less like a human being than I did in that moment when I confirmed my decision not to place you on life support. I could not really believe that I was betraying nearly seven years of helping you fight her cancer with tenacious will, spirit, and faith. I felt abjectly faithless, soulless, and godless.

CHAPTER FIFTY-SEVEN

Loss and Prayers

I don't remember our conversation in the car on the way to the hospital. I don't think many words were exchanged. I do recall that you had your arm around my shoulder and neck as I drove the forty-five minutes from Tehachapi to Bakersfield. Highway 58 was mostly vacant, save for the ever-present trucks. I don't remember blinking much, or breathing, or feeling anything physical except your arm and hand.

As we parked near the main hospital entrance, I whispered that this was going to be the roughest thing either of us had ever experienced. You responded, "I know, but Mom has been fighting so hard for so long. She deserves some peace."

As the elevator took us to the fifth floor, my heart dropped to a depth beyond my comprehension or imagination. As we walked past the nurses' station on our way to room 521, two nurses on duty looked at us with grief-stricken eyes. They didn't seem to be working or breathing. My heart sank even more, if that was possible.

The door to your room was partly closed. The privacy curtain had been pulled, blocking our entrance. Trent was behind me, and I sensed that he had started to cry before I pulled the curtain away. I began to cry as well.

You lay flat on your back. I could see the outline of your hands folded on your chest beneath the blanket and sheet. One of your nurses had humanely placed under your chin a towel, preventing your jaw from falling slack. I could see your eyes through your partly closed lids. To my eyes, your face always possessed an angelic quality, and this humble, unassuming sweetness still permeated your countenance. The Bell's palsy seemed finally gone. Where it had wrinkled unnaturally one side of your forehead, your skin now was smooth. Your lips, which had been pulled and twisted cruelly, exposing teeth and pulling one cheek back toward your ear, were now evenly together. The entire outline of your body beneath the blanket seemed frightfully small. Your swollen leg, the edema holding on even in death, still claimed most of the room in the bed.

Trent and I each hugged you and kissed you. Then we hugged each other and cried into each other's arms.

I prayed for forgiveness that I had not been with you when you died. I prayed that you had not suffered in your moments of dying. I prayed for your forgiveness that I had not been a better caregiver. I prayed that your soul would have a peaceful passage to heaven. I prayed that God would embrace you and let you know that in your battle against cancer, you had emulated his grace, faith, humility, and love. I prayed that God would heal your cancer as only he could. I prayed for the strength to support your sons in your absence. I prayed for the strength to honor your life and death and the dignity of your fight against cancer with whatever life I had left.

CHAPTER FIFTY-EIGHT

Departure

Trent and I kept a vigil for about two hours, and then it was time for him to say a final goodbye to his mom and return home to get some much-needed sleep. He had reached the point of physical and emotional collapse.

I had made several phone calls, first to Darlene's brother shortly after we had arrived at the hospital. Cary said that when the phone rang, he knew immediately its meaning. He said he was grateful that he was able to see Darlene before she passed. He would make the call to their parents in Indiana.

The plan all along had been for Cary to drive to LAX to pick up his wife and his brother Jeff, who were flying in from Texas and Pennsylvania, respectively, to see Darlene while she was being treated in the hospital. Now Cary's car ride had taken on a different meaning.

The call to John-Michael, who was attending college in Northridge, was gut-wrenching. How does one tell a son that his mother is dead? One simply says the words as gently and directly as one can. Leaving doubt for even a second seems more inhumane than delivering the news. John-Michael said he would get to the hospital as quickly as he could.

Between fits of crying and praying, I made calls to Darlene's closest friends. Each call was emotionally draining and at the same time healing. Darlene had the loveliest friends that one could possibly have. Her beautiful nature had allowed her to bond with angels here on earth. I will be eternally grateful for each word they shared with me as I sat alone next to Darlene's body.

John-Michael arrived at the hospital, cried and hugged me, and kept a vigil with Cary and me for a few hours. As John-Michael viewed his dead mother, I watched him experience an emotional disembowelment. Then I watched him reconstitute himself emotionally by fully embracing the memory of his alive mother and the reality of his dead mother and their twenty-five years of unconditional love. After several hours, John- Michael and Cary departed for LAX to pick up Tammey and Jeff.

Darlene had made arrangements to donate her body to medical research. She was also an organ donor. Because of her cancer, that meant corneas only. The research organization would pick up her body once her corneas had been taken.

Cary asked me to delay the cornea donation until he could return from LAX and allow his wife and brother a chance to say goodbye to Darlene.

At some point during the morning, I placed rosary beads over Darlene's hands.

As I sat at Darlene's beside, her oncologist from the cancer center showed up unexpectedly. He had no idea that Darlene had passed away. He was simply stopping by to see how Darlene was getting along in the hospital. I rose to my feet and informed him of what, as he entered the room, his own eyes had already gathered. He asked about what had transpired, and I gave him the details. I asked him if I had done the right thing in declining life-support measures. He said yes, that her body reached the limits of its temporal existence. He hugged me as I cried and struggled to accept his agreement with my judgment, still feeling as though I had let down my truest love. In a matter of minutes, he was gone, no doubt on his way to the cancer treatment center to treat other patients.

For the next several hours, I remained with Darlene in room 521. Nurses checked on me frequently. At one point, a nurse put drops in Darlene's eyes and taped her lids closed to preserve the worthiness of her corneas. At nearly noon, I was informed that Darlene's corneas needed to be harvested directly; otherwise, they would be of no use. I called Cary to see how close he was to arrival. Unfortunately, he was still hours away. I explained the urgency of the situation. He left the decision to me, and he graciously said he would explain things to his wife and brother; he assured me that they would understand. I let the nurse know she should proceed immediately.

The nurse told me that it would be best if I left the room. She needed to remove Darlene's catheter and generally prepare the body. She said I should spare myself seeing all that would be done; she reassured me that she would take special care in handling Darlene's body. Then she gave me a hug, which was more reassuring than her kind words.

In my hours with Darlene, I spoke to her when I wasn't praying. I tried to convey to her how much I loved her, how much I would always love her, how proud I was of her courageous fight against cancer, how I would persevere to honor her life with my life, how I would carry her in my heart for the rest of my life, how bravely her sons were coping, how much her sons loved her, how empty our lives would be without her.

The nurse helped me gather up Darlene's few belongings: her purse, her large bag of medicine and vitamins, her clothing, and her shoes. The nurse insisted that I take the six or seven bottles of Ensure that were scattered throughout the room.

The steps I needed to take to exit room 521 were the most miserable steps I had ever taken. I took them after giving Darlene one last embrace and sequence of kisses on her hands, which seemed now to be holding the rosary beads, her forehead, her cheeks, her chin, and her lips. I felt as though I were leaving myself as well as my beloved wife. Exiting the room, I fully felt someone other than whom I had been, married to Darlene.

CHAPTER FIFTY-NINE

Forever

After one of Darlene's final chemo treatments, she asked me if I knew how to get to the high school where Trent had an away soccer game. Darlene said she wanted to go to the game. I told her I could find the school, and she said, "Let's go."

We had to walk quite a distance from the parking lot to the stadium. Darlene held on to my arm with both of her hands and reminded me to walk slowly.

The weather could not have been more inhospitable to Darlene's physical condition. The blustery November winds showed no signs of abating. Dust swirls were making it difficult to see the field and the players. The late afternoon temperature was dropping quickly.

Once inside the stadium, we had to negotiate the metal bleachers. Darlene wrapped her arms around my waist and told me to take advantage of the handicap ramp. We settled in about three rows up. Darlene pulled her pink Polo cap hard down over her face. One eye was patched, as was the norm due to her Bell's palsy. We were both struggling against the stinging winds and swirling dust. The players on the field going against the wind were having a hard time advancing the ball. Trent was playing goalie.

Under calmer conditions, his kicks from the goal area would normally sail in the air far past the midline. Against the wind, he was lucky to advance the ball twenty yards.

Darlene fought the wind along with Trent and his teammates. She shouted words of encouragement with astonishing energy and volume, considering she had spent the better part of the day in the infusion center at the cancer center undergoing chemo. Fearful that the patch over her eye would not keep out all the dust, she used one hand as an additional shield. She rebuffed all my attempts to convince her that Trent would understand if we didn't stay for the entire game. We stayed for the whole game.

With our team losing 5–1, an opposing player wanted to fight Trent after a collision near our goal in which Trent caught the ball, and the other player got up looking for a fight. Trent ignored his threatening gestures and inappropriate language and waited patiently for the umpire to pull a yellow card. Darlene was not so serene in the stands. She jumped up and implored the umpire to pull a red card. Trent looked at his mother and shook his head no. He then extended his hands in Darlene's direction, palms downward, as if to say, "Calm down, Mom."

After the game, we joined Trent on the field to congratulate him and his teammates on a spirited game not only against the opposing team but also against the nature. Our team fought fiercely to the end despite the lopsided score. Darlene fought just as fiercely despite the lopsided score in her war against cancer.

Wind-swept, covered in dust, and shivering from the cold, Darlene and I made our way to the car, and her functioning eye and face radiated pride all the way home.

In Darlene's third year of fighting cancer, we drove with Trent to her hometown of Madison, Indiana, to visit her parents and childhood friends over the Christmas holidays. Darlene was at a point in her cancer war in which people were surprised that she actually had cancer. To look at her, one could not perceive physical signs of illness or debilitation.

Although we were hopeful that Darlene would overcome the challenges cancer presented, she was realistic about her future. She stated calmly that she wanted to visit her family and hometown while she was able to. As always, I tried to downplay her concerns, but I agreed that we should act while she felt healthy and in control of her disease. Darlene emphasized that she had friends that she wanted to see while she still looked like herself.

The drive cross-country from California to Madison, Indiana, is memorable in so many respects. Trent was a delight, commenting on the vast expanses of terrain in Arizona, New Mexico, Oklahoma, and Missouri. We had a winter storm following us east as we drove, but we managed to stay just ahead of it all the way to Madison. Trent and Darlene loved to stay up late, talking, laughing, and watching TV as I followed my usual pattern of "lights out" at 9:00 p.m. They joked about my snoring and took pictures of my silly sleeping postures and facial expressions. They also loved to sleep late, causing us to get underway at around noon each day. Consequently, we were still driving late into the night. I always took the first driving shift, as Darlene loved to drive at night with Trent as her navigator and me resting or sometimes napping in the back seat or reclining in the front seat. I would open my eyes to see Darlene at the wheel, listening to country music, softly singing to herself, or conversing with Trent about her childhood in Indiana, her brothers, college, and life in general. I loved seeing her at the wheel, fully in control, anxious to reunite with dear friends from her elementary and high school years, excited to show Trent and me the streets where she grew up, her schools, and the courts where she played tennis.

Darlene was so fully enthralled in her evening element, fully engaged in the night's charms of enchanting lights off in the distance, her son and husband close by, driving away from cancer, driving toward home. I could feel her hand holding mine or draped over my leg, assuring me that she was fully awake, feeling good enough to drive for several more hours, and comfortable with me closing my eyes, knowing that she had everything under control and believing that we had plenty of time ahead us.

Epilogue

✥

Acording to the American Cancer Society website, in 2016 doctors diagnosed an estimated 1,685,210 new cases of cancer in the United States. The ACS estimates that 595,690 cancer deaths occurred.

For 2015, the ACS estimates 231,840 cases of invasive breast cancer, meaning that cancer cells have spread beyond the walls of the breast's glands or ducts into nearby tissue and possibly other organs. The ACS estimates that in 2015, doctors treated 60,290 cases of in situ breast cancer, meaning that the cancer cells have not spread beyond the breast ducts. In 2015, the ACS estimates that 40,890 breast cancer patients succumbed to breast cancer.

The ACS estimates that 3.1 million women in the United States were battling some form of breast cancer as of January 2014. Among these women, a portion were cancer-free at that time, while others were showing evidence of active cancer cells, and still others were in treatment.

Again according the ACS data, the median age of a breast cancer patient at the time of diagnosis was 61, between the years 2008 and 2012. Currently in the United States, women face a 1 in 8 chance of being diagnosed with breast cancer during their lifetime. In the 1970s, the lifetime risk for women being diagnosed with breast cancer was 1 in 11. The ACS cites a variety of diverse influences to explain the increased incidence of breast cancer. These factors ironically include positive trends, such as the fact that people are living longer; some factors are negative, such as people being overweight.

The ACS estimates that in 2016, some form of cancer claimed the lives of 1,639 people each and every day. Only heart disease takes more lives than cancer. In 2016, cancer was responsible for almost 1 out of 4 deaths in the United States.

The soldiers who fight cancer did not volunteer for their mission. Cancer conscripted them with cruel, random indiscretion. Cancer's soldiers deserve all the care and compassion and support we can give them. As caregivers, however much we care and give, we must find a way to care and give more. Cancer is an enemy that exploits indifference and inaction. We must never allow people who are withstanding cancer's siege ever to feel that they are fighting alone.

Darlene taught me that the most important role we can play in this life is that of a caregiver. She cared for others as she herself suffered from and battled cancer. I have learned from Darlene's example that at all times, with or without cancer as our engaged enemy, we need to live with care, love with care, speak with care, act with care, remember with care, and imagine with care.

I cannot add color to the palette of Darlene's life and death. I can only try to see the bright, beautiful colors Darlene created and mixed and displayed in her fifty years of living. This book is my feeble attempt to do exactly that.

This book is also meant to be a Purple Heart for my wife who fought cancer bravely and honorably, without self-pity or self-indulgent martyrdom, and who ultimately gave her life in the war against cancer. Darlene demonstrated how to live every moment of life appreciably and joyfully, and she demonstrated how to die with dignity and without defeat.

Selfishly, this book also represents my need and desire to remain as close to Darlene as possible. The writing has served as a way for me to continue caring for my beloved wife. The writing is also an admission that Darlene taught me important lessons that I still need to learn.

The space Darlene's hospital bed occupied in our living room is space forever changed. The space looks and feels different. Sometimes, I move carefully around it, wanting to keep it inviolate, as it was when she was here. Other times, I am pulled into it, wanting to be infused and enveloped by it, sensing her very being in mine.

I look for signs in my everyday life—signs that Darlene is alive in another realm. Mornings when the sky presents pink hues that I've never noticed before—less orange and red—are my best days. Afternoons when the bull elk have gathered on the valley floor, reminding me that peace is an action of the heart, are my best days. Evenings when an owl talks to me, urging reflection upon all that Darlene shared, gifts of precise and infinite meaning, until I understand more deeply and lastingly, are my best days.

we danced
when you could not walk we prayed
when you could not talk we waited
when you could not feel your hands or feet we remembered
when you could not taste we embraced
when you could not sleep we provisioned
when you could not rise we confessed
when you could not follow we believed
when you could not swallow we promised
when you could not overcome we wept
when you could not wake

Obituary

❧

Darlene Rae Everidge-Coccari, of Tehachapi, California, left this world on October 1st after a nearly seven-year battle against breast cancer, during which she demonstrated great courage, grace, honor, optimism, and dignity, without ever losing her love of life, family, friends, co- workers, and students.

Darlene maintained her unfailing positive attitude toward life throughout her grueling fight against cancer. She felt that life was a precious gift from God; that living was a privilege and an opportunity to honor God. She was grateful for every moment of life and dedicated herself to making the world a better place.

While cancer undeniably robbed Darlene's body of strength, it utterly failed to touch or alter her beautiful soul, spirit, and mind.

Born in Madison, Indiana on April 7th, 1965, Darlene excelled in high school volleyball and tennis, earning a tennis scholarship to East Texas State University. She then transferred to and completed her scholarship at Texas State University in San Marcos. After earning her degree in English, she went to work as an Inventory Management Specialist first at Kelly Air Force Base in San Antonio, Texas and then at Edwards Air Force Base in California. After a 14-year stint working for the Federal Government with a classified security clearance, she decided to pursue a career in teaching.

After earning her teaching credential at Fresno State University, she began teaching in the Mojave Unified School District in Mojave,

California. During her 10-year teaching career, she demonstrated remarkable flexibility as she taught troubled students from ages seven to 13 in a self-contained setting, then junior high school English, math, and physical education, then kindergarten and second grade. Darlene loved all of her students, especially those facing daunting hardships in life. She donated or bought clothing for students who were without and worked tirelessly to ensure her students' success.

When Darlene's cancer had progressed to the point where she had to stop working, many of her colleagues in the district donated hundreds of hours of personal sick leave to Darlene to help her manage her illness and ease financial stress. These generous donations by her colleagues will forever remain a testament to her bright spirit and the positive impact she made on all those she worked with.

As a measure of Darlene's love of people, she has donated her corneas for transplanting to a sightless person and her body for medical research. Darlene was preceded in death by her grandparents, John W. and Charlotte Gullion; Grandmother Eloise Cowan Everidge Schnabel; Grandfather RB Everidge; Step-grandfather Melvin Schnabel.

Darlene is survived by her husband, Michael Coccari of Tehachapi; her son John-Michael, 24, of Northridge; her son Trent, 16, of Tehachapi; her parents, Michael D. and Phyllis D. Everidge of Madison, Indiana; brothers Michael W. Everidge and his wife Sharon of Austin, Indiana; Jeffrey and his wife Christina Everidge of Harrisburg, PA; Cary and his wife Tammye Everidge of Houston, Texas; nephews Zachery and Lucas Everidge of Harrisburg; Uncle John E. and Beverly Gullion of Scottsburg, Indiana; cousins Christy Deaton, Cara Alfele, Johnny Gullion, and Jonathan Gullion; sister and brother-in-law Judy and Roger Hough of Corona, CA; as well as the loving families of the Botbyls, St. Jeans, Smiths, and Branhams.

Memorial services are pending. Instead of sending flowers, anyone wanting to honor Darlene's memory is humbly asked to make a donation to the charity of your choice.

Memorial

D arlene has passed on to heaven, and we celebrate her undying love and brave spirit today, November 14, 2015, and forever in our hearts.

Darlene Rae Coccari left this world on October 1, 2015, to seek the healing hand of God in heaven. She did so after demonstrating how to live with love and compassion for all and how to die with grace, dignity, and wisdom.

Born on April 7, 1965, in Madison, Indiana, Darlene learned from her parents, brothers, friends, and teachers the Midwestern values of humility, hard work, loyalty, and integrity, and she humbly displayed and spread those values to everyone she encountered throughout her fifty years of blessed life.

Darlene first and foremost dedicated herself to her sons, John-Michael and Trent. She loved them unconditionally and worked every day to prepare them for life's most intense challenges and tribulations. As Darlene fought cancer with a ferocious spirit and undaunted will, she was inspired by her sons' emotional maturation and intellectual development and always sought one more hug, one more conversation, one more opportunity to say "I love you." She wisely counseled them about how to reconcile her death and live honorably with a mother who would forever remain in their hearts.

Darlene did not have friends so much as she had spiritual sisters and brothers. She considered it her privilege to know and love her spiritual sisters and brothers with undying respect and devotion.

The earthly cause that Darlene remained committed to until her final breath was the well-being of her family. She thought about and prayed for her parents and three biological brothers—Mike, Jeff, and Cary—every day that I knew her. Geographical distance from her family pained her, but Darlene kept all her family members emotionally close in her mind and heart with religious conviction.

Darlene loved life as a precious gift from God. She loved profoundly and deeply all the people in her life, including her students from her decade of teaching, with admiration, respect, and wholehearted commitment to their happiness, safety, and well-being.

No one can properly explain how much mental, physical, and spiritual strength Darlene showed as she battled cancer. She never felt sorry for herself; she never became bitter. She never played the victim. She never lost her sense of humor; she never let go of her sense of optimism. Darlene never allowed cancer to compromise or diminish her love of life. Cancer is weaker for having chosen Darlene as an opponent.

Darlene left us with so many important lessons: live without ego, love people with open arms and an open heart, make the world a better place for our children, regard every moment of life as a sacred blessing from God, remain forever positive, forgive enemies with compassion, stay strong when weakness beckons, and trust and embrace God's plan even when we don't fully understand it.

Heaven has one more angel who loves us still.

Darlene with her brothers Mike, Jeff, and Cary

Darlene with her sons John-Michael and Trent

Darlene and Michael

Darlene Rae Coccari

CPSIA information can be obtained
at www.ICGtesting.com
Printed in the USA
BVHW050753221022
650026BV00001B/35